Helen Whitaker Fowle

Mary Scott

Mrs.

Dottie Martin

Jessie Rae Scott

Mrs. R. G. Cherry

Merle Davis Umstead

Carolyn Hunt

Eleanor Kearny Carr

Fanny Y. Bickett

Alice W. Broughton

Angelia

Mildred.

Nina Deadirick Glenn.

Martha B. Hodges

Jessie Rae Scott

Mrs. T. W. Bick

Mrs. James B. Hunt Jr.

Mrs. James G. Martin

North Carolina's First Ladies

1891–2001

North Carolina's First Ladies
1891–2001

Who Have Resided in the

Executive Mansion

At 200 North Blount Street

MARIE SHARPE HAM

DEBRA A. BLAKE AND C. EDWARD MORRIS

BASED ON
the 1981 and 1987 editions of
The First Ladies of North Carolina
Written by Jeanelle Coulter Moore
and Grace Rutledge Hamrick

PUBLISHED BY
The Executive Mansion Fine Arts Committee
and The Executive Mansion Fund, Inc.
2000

PRINTED IN THE UNITED STATES OF AMERICA

ISBN 0-86526-294-2

This book is dedicated to

First Lady Carolyn Leonard Hunt

for her interest in having the history of these first ladies preserved and recorded so that others might know and respect each of their special and unique styles.

In addition, this book is dedicated to the memory and devotion that the original authors,

Jeanelle Coulter Moore and
Grace Rutledge Hamrick,

gave to the research and writings.

Contents

Foreword

It is a privilege to write the foreword to this new edition of *North Carolina's First Ladies, 1891–2001*. The women we honor in this volume stood side by side with their husbands, our governors, through all of North Carolina's proud history—in good times and in bad, in joy and in sorrow, in triumph and in tragedy. They were mentors and leaders, helpmates and hostesses, wives, mothers, daughters, sisters, and friends. They came from all areas of our state, from across the country, and even—during the colonial era—from around the world. Each brought her unique and wonderful talents to the roles she played in North Carolina's story.

Little was written about these women specifically until the late Jeanelle Coulter Moore, wife of the late governor and associate justice of North Carolina's Supreme Court Dan K. Moore, acknowledged the lack of information about the First Ladies and their roles and service to the state. Earlier research and interviews had been undertaken by Marjorie Spruill and Beth G. Crabtree; Sam Ragan, first secretary of the Department of Art, Culture and History (presently Department of Cultural Resources), had provided guidance and resources. Mrs. Moore recruited the late Grace Rutledge Hamrick (Mrs. Rush Hamrick) of Shelby to write a book about the First Ladies of North Carolina. Grace Hamrick was a fine writer and an expert editor; she undertook the research and composition of the first edition, which was published in 1981 during the tenure of Secretary of Cultural Resources Sara W. Hodgkins. The first edition sold out quickly, and a second edition was undertaken and completed in 1987 during Secretary Patric G. Dorsey's tenure. That edition, too, sold out quickly and, hence, this revised edition, which is much more comprehensive than its two predecessors. These publications tell the stories of the First Ladies from 1891, when the current Executive Mansion was completed. The revised edition has added a photographic essay of earlier First Ladies.

All of these women served the state of North Carolina in many ways that reflected and expressed their talents, opportunities, and special insights. As the roles and responsibilities of women have changed over the past one hundred years, the First Ladies of the state have been remarkably consistent in their commitment to public action. That commitment was, to be sure, expressed in different ways, but it was characterized by the understanding that—even without a constitutional basis—being a First Lady was a public office. That is, the people of North Carolina were to be served in actions that called attention to public issues not so much in a partisan way but in a manner that reflected interests and commitments of women. I have known many First Ladies of the state, but it has been my honor and deep personal satisfaction to work most closely with Carolyn Leonard Hunt, whose tenure has been marked by many achievements on behalf of *all* the people.

We are proud of and grateful to our First Ladies for their signal leadership and many contributions. This book is one way in which to thank them for all they have meant to North Carolina.

By Betty Ray McCain, *Secretary*
North Carolina Department of Cultural Resources

Preface

It has been thirteen years since the publication of the second edition of *The First Ladies of North Carolina*. The original concept of such a history came from the late first lady Jeanelle Coulter Moore, widow of Governor Dan K. Moore, who initiated the Executive Mansion Fine Arts Committee and made countless rich contributions to the life of the state. Mrs. Moore felt that the first ladies should be personalized, sensing that a volume about their lives would pay tribute to their service to the state. The co-author and editor with Mrs. Moore was the late Grace Hamrick, a distinguished journalist. The first edition was confined to those first ladies who had lived in the mansion on Blount Street, starting with Miss Helen Fowle. Mrs. Hunt has been anxious to have the book updated since more historic information has come to light in the past few years. It seems not only an appropriate but also a magical time to have a new edition.

Under the leadership of Mrs. Hunt, many beautiful objects have been added to the mansion from gifts and its endowment income. Mrs. Hunt has been enthusiastic about discovering original artworks by North Carolina artists in particular and adding period furnishings from the South, especially from our state. She and the Executive Mansion Fine Arts Committee felt it important to form a collection of those pieces for the mansion, and they have added greatly to the cultural atmosphere of the various rooms.

The members of the Executive Mansion Fine Arts Committee have enjoyed every moment of working with Mrs. Hunt. We have had mutual fun expressing ideas, then watching them grow into picture-book furnishings. We have been anxious to express our gratitude to her for being so gracious and responsive. Knowing of her enthusiasm for all facets of the history of the Executive Mansion and its occupants, we have dedicated this book to Carolyn Hunt, who has been first lady for a record number of years. In the midst of assisting Governor Hunt in countless ways, officiating at public functions, caring for their young family, volunteering in the public schools, and running the family farm, she has found time to work with the Executive Mansion Fine Arts Committee in beautifying the glorious, historic landmark. In addition to all of that, she has inspired the documentation of the lives of the first ladies of North Carolina.

Mrs. Hunt's kindness and charm are beguiling. In her quiet, sweet way, she makes all North Carolinians, as well as visitors, feel at home. One senses in her an absolute devotion to the Executive Mansion as a warm, welcoming home reaching out to the people of the state.

By Mary Duke Biddle Trent Semans, *Chairman*
Executive Mansion Fine Arts Committee

Acknowledgments

This book was made possible by the effort and interest of many people, each of whom demonstrated a personal commitment to historical accuracy in the portrayals of the lives of the volume's twenty-six subjects.To all of those committed, resourceful people goes our sincere gratitude. Assistance rendered by the Department of Cultural Resources began at the top. Secretary Betty Ray McCain and Deputy Secretary Elizabeth F. Buford, along with staff members, notably Donna Rosefield, as well as Kelli Barham and Jennifer McCrory, have cooperated in every way to make this project a priority and to make available every necessary resource.

The Division of Archives and History has been deeply involved: Dr. Jeffrey J. Crow, director, and David J. Olson, deputy director; Catherine J. Morris, Jesse R. Lankford Jr., Kim Cumber, Carol Campbell, Paul Dasinger, G. Ed Southern, Jason Tomberlin, Ron Vestal, and Ansley Wegner; Bill Garrett, Bob Harrelson, Earl Ijames, Steve Massengill, and Alan Westmoreland; Ken Simpson and Mark Valsame; Dr. Jerry C. Cashion, Dr. Jerry Cross, and Mike Hill; Druscilla Simpson and Mark Moore; and the staff of the Historical Publications Section.

Management and staff of the State Library of North Carolina were of invaluable assistance: Steven Case, Frank Holt, Cynthia Jones, Sandra Lovely, Cheryl McLean, Alma Perry, Denise Sigmon, Angie Suhr, Pam Toms, and Debby Whitley. The North Carolina Museum of History provided access to research and files on its 1997 exhibition *First Families of North Carolina*. Thanks go to Janice C. Williams, the museum's interim director, as well as Dr. Vicki Berger, Louise Benner, Eric Blevins, Paige Myers, Kent Thompson, and Linda Williams. We also appreciate the assistance of Dr. Lawrence J. Wheeler, director of the North Carolina Museum of Art, and that of Barbara Wiedemann, Heather Hensley, and Katie Massey.

The following historic sites provided useful information: Aycock Birthplace, Fremont; Blandwood Mansion, Greensboro; Bracebridge Hall, Edgecombe County; Hope Plantation, Windsor; House in the Horseshoe, Moore County; Tryon Palace Historic Sites & Gardens, New Bern; and the Zebulon B. Vance Birthplace, Weaverville. The following educational and cultural institutions provided assistance: Alamance Community College, Graham; the Alamance County Historical Museum, near Burlington; the Duke University Special Collections Library, Durham; the East Carolina Manuscript Collection and the Special Collections of Joyner Library at East Carolina University, Greenville; the Haw River Historical Museum, Haw River; the Museum of Early Southern Decorative Arts, Winston-Salem; the New Hanover County Library, Wilmington; St. Mary's School, Raleigh; the University of North Carolina at Greensboro; and the Wake County Library Regional Historical Collection, Raleigh.

Special thanks to Robert G. Anthony and staff of the North Carolina Collection, University of North Carolina Library, Chapel Hill, and Timothy Pyatt and staff of the Southern Historical Collection (also at UNC–CH).

Numerous individuals rendered invaluable help, among them William Bushong, Nancy Covington, Dylan Morris, Millie Ravenel, Sylvia Ray, and Dennis Toney. Many former first ladies or their descendants participated in this project by offering information or illustrations or agreeing to read preliminary drafts of the text. Their contributions are evident, and we extend our sincere appreciation.

Without the abiding and dedicated professionalism of Debra A. Blake and C. Edward Morris this book would not be possible. We are tremendously grateful to Janice D. Shearin, executive assistant to First Lady Carolyn Hunt, for her assistance at every stage of this project.

Special thanks go to Chairman Mary Duke Biddle Trent Semans (Mrs. James H. Semans), the entire Executive Mansion Fine Arts Committee, the Executive Mansion Fund, Inc., and the Mary Duke Biddle Foundation for their generous funding of this edition and their constant and capable care of the 1891 Executive Mansion. They have dedicated this edition of *North Carolina's First Ladies, 1891–2001* to Mrs. Carolyn Leonard Hunt with admiration for a lifetime of devoted service to the people of our great state.

Introduction

The authors, editors, and publishers hope that readers of this volume will become intrigued with the twenty-six first ladies who have resided in North Carolina's Executive Mansion since 1891—women who have served their beloved state with devotion, dedication, creativity, and dignity. Every effort has been made to present new information and examine more fully the lives of these women, who assumed their official roles by virtue of their husbands' election to public office. Many of them would have preferred to continue their roles as wives and mothers in the comfort and relative privacy of their own homes; still others would have preferred to pursue their chosen careers out of the spotlight. Nonetheless, all accepted the role of first lady with pride and conviction. The reader will find all of them to be unique in the ways they went about the tasks expected of them and in the plans and projects they chose to undertake. Each woman accepted her role and individualized her time as first lady, responding to various circumstances and making her contributions where and as she could.

In the more than thirty years since this work was conceived, much has been recognized about women's roles in society, and people are more eager to know what the women of past generations were like. Women who have been in the public eye or "on stage" are of particular interest; indeed, their enhanced visibility offers a readily comprehensible aspect of their respective generation and place in history. By studying such women, one is able to identify the many similarities (as well as the glaring differences) between their lives and the lives most women lead at present. Our only wish is that we could have had more time to research our subjects further and to present a more thorough view of them. There are a few first ladies about whom relatively little is known; many inspired in us the desire to have known them personally.

This newest publication has been enlarged to incorporate images that further illuminate some of the varied roles these women undertook. The illustrations represent windows through which readers might glimpse a more accurate picture of the character of these women and the nature of their roles as first lady. The book reveals that their lives were not always glamorous or limited to attendance at social functions but were instead substantial, sometimes involving unexpected or unimagined activities. Some played harmonicas, picked up trash from alongside highways, portrayed historical figures; others promoted agricultural products or kept gardens to help supply food for the mansion.

Our quest for information and understanding remains keen. It is our hope that additional material will emerge to reveal an even more complete picture of each woman. But for now, we are confident that this volume will not only help readers know many of North Carolina's first ladies better but also inspire admiration for the way they responded to the role that destiny dictated for them.

by Marie Sharpe Ham
Publication Director

The Governor's Executive Mansion

AT 200 NORTH BLOUNT STREET
1883–2001

Now more than a century old, the Victorian house familiar to North Carolinians as the Governor's Mansion is a historic monument that embodies in its architecture the state's late-nineteenth-century striving for economic modernization. Built in the "gingerbread" Queen Anne style, the house was an ambitious manifestation of the state's transition from the arduous economic recovery following the Civil War to a new era of progress marked by rapid industrial development, the construction of rail networks, and movement of people from the farm to the factory.

The building, designed in 1883, was one of the first examples of the Queen Anne style in North Carolina, a picturesque architecture expressive of the technological possibilities and the newfound industrial wealth of the age. The mansion's Queen Anne character is readily displayed in its steeply pitched roofs, richly colored textural surfaces, porches and pavilions, projecting patterned chimneys, and elaborate mass-produced turned porch woodwork.

Although built as a symbol of late-nineteenth-century progress and the spirit of the "New South," the Executive Mansion also incorporates the aspirations and styles of later generations. Its interior was significantly altered to a Beaux-Arts decor in the 1920s, reflecting both a change in architectural taste and the expansion of formal entertainment attached to the office of governor. In the 1970s, when a decision was made to retain the house as the official executive residence after years of public discussion concerning possible demolition or use as a museum, another significant rehabilitation took place. The successful movement to preserve the mansion has underscored its status in recent times as an emblem of state pride. Over the past one hundred years, the house has evolved into a "living institution" and an invaluable asset to the state.

PREVIOUS RESIDENCES

The history of an official governor's residence dates from the colonial past. Starting with the construction of Governor William Tryon's New Bern house in 1767, North Carolinians have intermittently struggled to define what was an appropriate residence for the chief executive. Tryon Palace, designed by English architect John Hawks and built between 1767 and 1770, became one of the most admired public structures in North America. The elegant Palladian residence did not, however, please the farmers of North Carolina's backcountry counties, who resented the payment of additional taxes to defray the cost of its construction. Although Governor Tryon had expected the Georgian-style house to serve as the executive residence for generations, its official use was brief. The Revolutionary War ended the residence's status as a provincial palace, and official business was conducted there during the early years of statehood. In 1798 the central block and east wing were destroyed by fire. The present structure, a popular historic attraction in its own right, is largely a 1950s reconstruction based on archaeological research and Hawks's original plans.

The next official residence for the state's chief executive was not established until the legislature, after years of controversy and indecision, finally established Raleigh as the state capital in 1792. In 1797 a frame residence (no longer extant) at the corner of Fayetteville and Hargett Streets was purchased for the first family. Although it was one of the finest buildings in Raleigh at that time, the structure was scorned by some visitors, and it soon proved inadequate for the governor's requirements. The legislature periodically considered selling the property and erecting a new gubernatorial residence, but no action was taken until 1813.

Construction of what became known as the Governor's Palace began during the War of 1812, and the building was completed in 1816 by Boston builder James Calder at a cost of approximately ten thousand dollars. The impressive two-story porticoed Classical Revival brick structure set an early stylistic tone for much of Raleigh's antebellum public architecture. Between 1816 and 1865 the Governor's Palace was the official residence of twenty governors. The house subsequently served as Union general William T. Sherman's Raleigh headquarters during his Civil War campaign in the state and later became the headquarters of the military commandant of North Carolina. By the end of the Reconstruction era, the house was in a deteriorated condition and considered no longer suitable for the governor's residence. The state leased the building to various tenants and later sold the property to the Raleigh public school board. In 1885 the palace was razed and the Centennial School was built on the site. The school was removed in 1932 to make way for Raleigh Memorial Auditorium.

Until 1891, when the present mansion was first occupied, many of North Carolina's governors of the post-Civil War years were obliged to reside in rented houses or respected hostelries such as the Yarborough House. Governor Thomas J. Jarvis, a self-made man and a tough, pragmatic politician, championed the erection of the new residence. The General Assembly flatly denied his first request in 1881, but that did not deter Jarvis. The governor lobbied aggressively for the Governor's Mansion, assuring legislators that it could be built cheaply. He appealed to state pride in his 1883 biennial message to the legislature, earnestly stating, "It does not comport with the dignity of the State for the Governor to live at a hotel, where he is unable to dispense the hospitality incumbent upon him and due to the State, to say nothing of the personal inconvenience to himself." The General Assembly eventually responded to the governor's persuasive economic arguments and his appeal to state patriotism and authorized the construction of the new governor's residence, providing that the mansion's construction, when possible, use labor and materials furnished by the North Carolina State Penitentiary. In May 1883 the governor and his Council of State entered into a contract with the penitentiary to build the residence for the sum of twenty-five thousand dollars.

THE ARCHITECTS AND BUILDER

The nationally renowned Philadelphia architect Samuel Sloan (1815–1884) and his young assistant, Adolphus G. Bauer (1858–1898), prepared plans and specifications for the new house. In 1883 Sloan was in the waning years of an illustrious career during which he designed numerous residences, churches, commercial buildings, schools, and more than thirty state psychiatric hospitals throughout the United States. Sloan regularly visited Raleigh after 1875 to report on the construction of his commission for the Western Insane Asylum in Morganton, presently known as the Western Carolina Center. Impressed by the architect's credentials, Governor Jarvis in April 1883 selected Sloan to design the mansion and aided the architect in obtaining further public design work in the state. The mansion and several other projects were in progress when Sloan died unexpectedly on July 19, 1884.

After Sloan's death his twenty-five-year-old apprentice, A. G. Bauer, completed many of Sloan's commissions. Bauer later settled in North Carolina and became one of the state's most important late-nineteenth-century architects. He achieved notoriety for his flamboyant Queen Anne-style buildings such as the extant North Carolina School for the Deaf in Morganton (1892) and the Lucy Capehart House in Raleigh (1897). Bauer's personal life was tinged with romance and tragedy, and the tale of his love for an Indian "princess" is now the subject of local legend. He courted and married the Indian maiden Rachel Blythe in 1895, disregarding a state anti-miscegenation law and defying his family. Bauer was later racked by debilitating bouts of depression caused by a head injury suffered in a railroad accident and Rachel's unexpected death after the birth of their second child. Those melancholy moods ruined his promising career, and in 1898 Bauer ended his life in a Raleigh hotel room with a single pistol shot to the head.

The man ultimately responsible for the mansion's successful construction was Colonel William Jackson Hicks (1827–1911), a skilled contractor and excellent administrator. Hicks was an important figure in government service as the appointed architect and warden of the state penitentiary. He held that position from 1872 until his retirement in 1894, managing the state penitentiary and supervising the construction of state buildings in Raleigh. Hicks also served as an expert adviser for the state's proposed building projects, and he may have played a key role in the official choice of architects.

"JARVIS'S FOLLY"

On the morning of August 3, 1883, a stockade "nine feet high and quite substantial," designed to keep a large daily force of convict laborers at the building site, began to rise on the periphery of Burke Square. Soon after the erection of that stockade, Burke Square became a busy construction site, and the Raleigh *News and Observer* predicted that the new Executive Mansion would be rapidly completed. Such did not prove to be the case.

The first official construction report, prepared by William J. Hicks in 1884, was a glowing description of the structure's progress, describing the newly roofed fine-pressed brick-

Southwest view of Executive Mansion ca. 1895

Grand Hallway in the Executive Mansion ca. 1895

and-sandstone building as a "handsome design" of the "best material and workmanship." Hicks reported that the efficient labor force was made up almost entirely of convicts who had made the bricks, cut the stone, milled the lumber, and provided the labor for the few brickmasons and carpenters employed to direct the skilled work on the house. Bad news in the form of itemized construction costs that totaled $27,724.73 concluded the report. The building fund of nearly thirty thousand dollars collected to date from the sale of public lands in Raleigh was nearly depleted. With funds running low, construction slowed, then virtually stopped. Plastering, glazing, and other minor work continued, but the substantial interior and exterior ornamental woodwork could not be installed without additional funding. In April 1887 the mansion was closed and construction halted. By the end of the year, the vacant and forlorn building on Burke Square was becoming known as "Jarvis's Folly."

Even under Hicks's expert supervision, the cost of the Executive Mansion far exceeded the contracted amount of twenty-five thousand dollars for completion of the building. Changes in the structure's design, construction delays, and uncertainty caused by political opposition made the building campaign difficult. Fortunately, Governor Daniel G. Fowle pushed for completion of the building with additional revenues received in 1889 from the sale of land owned by the state. Although still not completed, the mansion was quickly made ready for occupancy by Fowle and his family in January 1891 at a cost of $58,843.01.

The legislature's steadfast refusal from 1885 to 1889 to appropriate state funds for the mansion had roots in a populist sentiment prevalent in rural North Carolina. Legislators representing the state's disgruntled farmers had voiced early opposition to the residence. Many saw the construction of a fine mansion as pretentious and inconsistent with republican agrarian values and fiscal conservatism. In 1883 the Raleigh *Farmer and Mechanic*, an aggressive voice of agrarian interests in North Carolina, sourly predicted that the building would cost the state one hundred thousand dollars to erect and furnish. When construction of the mansion began, the newspaper caustically stated: "a state which has the largest number of persons unable to read and write has no need for purple and fine linens." Populist grievances, symptomatic of much larger economic and social issues facing the state in the 1880s—issues such as demands for railroad regulation, better crop prices, and improvements in rural education—were never far from the surface and prolonged opposition to the Executive Mansion.

Photographs taken about 1895 during the administration of Elias Carr capture the exuberant high Victorian character of the residence as it appeared just after its completion. The mansion's porches and trim were originally painted a soft medium green with decorative bands of dark green and reddish brown. The window sash was also reddish brown, and the porches had light rose ceilings and gray-brown floors. This Victorian color scheme was changed when the woodwork was painted a uniform pinkish beige in the 1930s. Various colored stained-glass panes that once bordered the tall plate-glass "Queen Anne windows" were replaced with clear glass during that period. The building's exterior has lost little of its ornament except for lattice-style panels and sawn brackets from the porches. The only major change made to the exterior since its construction has been the enclosing of porches on the north and east sides to expand the kitchen and security facilities and to provide a Breakfast Room and Morning Room.

The first-floor plan of the mansion has not changed substantially since the 1890s, and the ease with which that layout adjusts to public or private uses remains a frequently praised attribute today. The large central hall runs from east to west and divides the major public rooms of the building. A secondary hall on the north side of the house runs north to south and separates the Ladies' Parlor and the Dining Room on the north side of the Grand Hallway. On the south side of the central hall are the Gentlemen's Parlor, the Ballroom, and the Library. The spacious rooms and central cross hall provide the circulation needed for large receptions, dinners, or social gatherings. Yet the second-floor quarters are private and set apart from the almost daily traffic of meetings, charity events, and tour groups.

The interior of the house received a neoclassic makeover by the Durham architectural firm of Atwood and Nash in 1925 during the administration of Angus W. McLean. The high Victorian character of the house, defined by the brown hues and texture of the heart-pine paneling and wainscoting and the monumental heart-pine-and-oak staircase, was rendered less formidable by ivory paint. The original effect of the heart-pine interior can be visualized today by examining the restored woodwork of the massive staircase and the doors and paneling of the library. Governor McLean's renovators also removed Victorian columns and balustrades from the Grand Hallway and substituted the Corinthian columns seen there today. Those changes had the cumulative effect of creating brighter, airy spaces as the backdrop for the neoclassic design considered tasteful and elegant in the 1920s. That mixture of Victorian and neoclassic styles has defined the overall architectural character of the building ever since.

A NORTH CAROLINA INSTITUTION

Within a generation the Executive Mansion's architecture would be considered old-fashioned, but the solid walls and utilitarian spaces survived alteration and the threat of demolition. In 1970 the mansion was listed in the National Register of Historic Places, and, shortly thereafter, public opposition scotched a proposal to build a new executive residence in suburban Raleigh. In 1974–1975 the state completed a major systems renovation and rehabilitation of the building's architecture. That extensive work, although visually inconspicuous, was vital to the preservation and continued use of the building.

In retrospect, three vital characteristics have ensured the house's longevity and recognition as a state landmark. First and foremost, it was and remains an outstanding facility for entertainment. Governor Fowle immediately demonstrated that aspect of the house with an opening gala reception for two thousand people in 1891. On the other hand, the mansion is well suited as a setting for smaller gatherings, and dinners at the residence appear to have had a special charm of their own. Governor O. Max Gardner, for example, desiring to promote a state program to encourage increased independent production of crops by North Carolina's farmers, in 1929 hosted a special "live-at-home" feast for more than a dozen of the state's newspaper editors. The menu consisted entirely of Tar Heel food products, including Hyde County oysters; Mount Olive pickles; mountain turkeys from North Wilkesboro; and hams, potatoes, yams, and turnip greens from state prison farms. The dinner was said to have been one of Governor Gardner's most eloquent political statements.

In recent years, Governor and Mrs. James E. Holshouser Jr. likewise used the building as a persuasive setting, hosting a series of "leadership" dinners in the ballroom during sessions of the General Assembly. Those social functions facilitated exchange between state legislators and prominent professionals in such fields as banking, industry, science, and education. The dinners are said to have led to the introduction of important bills in the General Assembly. Executive Mansion dinners do not always have political overtones and on many occasions simply provide relaxed merriment. Governor and Mrs. Locke Craig hosted an infamous dinner party that led to a dishpan ride down the mansion's main stairs by the guest of honor, Louise Wise, daughter of oil baron and real estate developer Henry Flagler. Well known for their sense of humor, Governor and Mrs. Robert W. Scott immensely enjoyed hosting elegant black-tie hog-chitlin-and-possum dinners for friends and associates at the mansion.

Every first lady undertakes responsibility for the entertaining associated with the office of governor. In 1919 Mrs. Thomas W. Bickett forcefully directed the legislature's attention to that aspect of the mansion's importance in a letter requesting funds for the building's renovation. She wrote: "The Mansion is an Institution, and not simply a residence. The governor

Southwest view of the Executive Mansion

and his wife are the representatives of the State, and are called upon to dispense the State's hospitality. The governor's wife, as his wife, is expected to extend the hospitality of the state to distinguished visitors from our own as well as other states, to entertain, to return her calls, and to discharge many social obligations that do not devolve upon a private individual."

The first ladies who succeeded Mrs. Bickett shared her views and at times struggled with the high expectations and ever increasing social duties. It was not until the administration of Governor Luther Hodges that civic and business groups and school groups were required to schedule their teas, receptions, and tours. Until then, it was assumed that the first lady would be available to serve as the hostess for teas or tours on short notice.

Fine southern hospitality at the mansion has been considered essential to the state's image from the earliest times. Although they were visitors before or after their terms of office, Presidents William Howard Taft, Calvin Coolidge, Franklin D. Roosevelt, and Harry S. Truman were honored guests at the mansion, as were Vice President and Mrs. Walter Mondale and first ladies Rosalynn S. Carter and Barbara P. Bush. A variety of famous show business personalities, including the opera diva Lily Pons and actors Katharine Hepburn, Alan Alda, Arnold Schwarzenegger, Gregory Peck, Lauren Bacall, Holly Hunter, Danny Aiello, and Natalie Wood, have likewise attended functions or performed in movies filmed at the house. During both world wars, the mansion provided the setting for dinners and receptions held to express appreciation to servicemen for their participation in those conflicts. Many North Carolinians donated food ration coupons out of concern that shortages might adversely affect the state's hospitality at the mansion!

Grand Hallway of the Executive Mansion

A second characteristic has been the mansion's easy conversion into a comfortable haven for private business meetings or bipartisan discourse concerning legislation or decision-making. Some of the earliest negotiations that led to the creation of the Research Triangle Park were held between Governor Luther Hodges and New York textile manufacturer Karl Robbins over business luncheons and dinners at the mansion. Governor James B. Hunt Jr. particularly valued the mansion's utility as an extension of his office at the Capitol, serving among other uses as a regular meeting place for the governor's personal staff, his cabinet, and the Council of State. Governor James G. Martin used the house as a "conference center" where private meetings for budget discussions, scheduling, and legislative strategy were held. From Governor Hodges to the present, the residence has served North Carolina well as a place to negotiate matters of public policy affecting the state.

Possibly the mansion's most important attribute has been its role as a symbol of the state's historic and cultural heritage. The building's now widespread recognition as an important historic structure is a relatively recent phenomenon that can be traced to the period just after World War II. Henry L. Kamphoefner, the young dean of the North Carolina State College School of Design, provided Governor W. Kerr Scott a report on the house in 1949 as part of preparations for a substantial renovation. Dean Kamphoefner brought several members of the School of Design faculty with him on an inspection tour of the house. Among the architectural experts was Lewis Mumford, an eminent architectural critic for the *New York Times* and an expert on cultural history. The overall content of the report can be summarized in Mumford's reaction to the building. In Mumford's view, expressed at a time when historic Victorian architecture was rarely appreciated by architects or the public, the mansion was "entitled to the same kind of respect we would pay a building done one hundred years earlier for it represents the living history of the State of North Carolina. In approaching such a monument, the utmost care should be taken to preserve and enhance the value of all that is worth being preserved—not to demolish the existing structure, or to hide it behind a facade of a quite different age and state of culture." As it turned out, a subsequent appropriation of fifty thousand dollars to renovate the mansion proved insufficient for a full-scale refurbishing project, but Kamphoefner and his faculty fostered among state officials a newfound respect for the mansion that ultimately enabled the building to be preserved in an era during which many Victorian structures were being remodeled or demolished.

The mansion's symbolic importance to the modern cultural history of North Carolina was underscored by Governor and Mrs. Terry Sanford, who promoted the advancement of culture in the state by holding events at the mansion that benefited such groups as the North Carolina School of the Arts and the North Carolina Symphony. The governor and his wife, Margaret Rose, also maintained an open-door social policy at the mansion. The popularity of mansion tours by schoolchildren visiting the state capital increased sharply during the Sanford administration, as did the mansion's use as a venue for charitable events and social causes.

Governor Dan K. Moore and his wife Jeanelle recognized the public's growing recognition of the historical and cultural significance of the mansion and enthusiastically set out to institutionalize a plan to preserve and maintain the house. The result of their efforts was 1967 legislation that created the Executive Mansion Fine Arts Commission (EMFAC), which has functioned since that time as an advisory board for the mansion's preservation and maintenance needs. Over the years, EMFAC has provided an important service to the state in advising the first family on periodic interior design changes. The scope of the committee's responsibilities expanded in 1989 when a comprehensive landscape plan was instituted. A highlight of that plan was the creation of a Victorian-style garden, financed by private contributions, as both a complement to and an outdoor extension of the South Porch and Ballroom.

In 1969 Governor and Mrs. Robert W. Scott found living conditions in the mansion to be less than accommodating for them and their five children. The poor conditions led Governor Scott to suggest that it might be time to build a new residence, even though he preferred the present one; but he realized that the house needed extensive repairs and upgrading of the mechanical systems for it to be a comfortable home. The General Assembly created an Executive Residence Building Commission to investigate and suggest a solution to the situation. The commission's findings eventually led to legislative appropriations in the amount of $854,000 to renovate the building. It fell to Governor and Mrs. James E. Holshouser Jr. to oversee the most extensive work done on the mansion since its original construction. Mrs. Pat Holshouser stated: "Our determination to emphasize North Carolina products clearly carries through the theme that Governor Jarvis had when he first envisioned a new Executive Mansion."

The first two terms of Governor James B. Hunt Jr. saw a continuation of that same spirit. Numerous projects were undertaken to further improve the mansion for its visitors and residents. The most significant one involved restoring the heart-pine woodwork to its original stained finish in the library and replacing most of the furnishings. Mrs. Carolyn Hunt expanded the interpretative history programs through tours that included preschool children and handicapped and foreign visitors.

Governor and Mrs. James G. Martin, with the support and assistance of former first ladies, a professional fund raiser, and EMFAC, not only raised more than one million dollars as an endowment for the mansion but also, with state senator Kenneth Royall's backing, persuaded the General Assembly to authorize a one-million-dollar matching grant. That endowment, designated as the Executive Mansion Fund, Inc., is used to preserve and maintain the house and its furnishings for years to come. Moreover, for the first time the position of curator of the Executive Mansion was established, and a historical video and hardback book on the official residence were produced.

Governor and Mrs. Hunt's devotion to the mansion and state continued during their unprecedented third and fourth terms. Through their commitment to children and education, mansion tours focusing on the deaf and visually impaired have been incorporated and touring opportunities expanded. For the first time, the massive roof was totally replaced using the existing pattern, shape, and colors of slate. A collection of southern and North Carolina period antiques has been added.

As the mansion continues into its second century, the house embodies both the vigor and optimism of the time of its construction and a traditional attachment to conservative architecture and decor. When proposed, it was, in the words of Thomas J. Jarvis, to be both "beautiful and cheap." More than one hundred years later, most North Carolinians would agree that the Executive Mansion is a handsome residence and that it is an invaluable asset to the state.

North Carolina now has one of the few governor's residences in the nation constructed in the nineteenth century and still in continuous use. The Executive Mansion reflects the past and stands solidly to face the future. Over the years, the time, talent, funds, and devotion of North Carolinians have contributed to its unending tradition of gracious hospitality to all who enter its doors.

Researched and written by William Bushong and Marie Sharpe Ham
Revised by Marie Sharpe Ham

Helen Whitaker Fowle (Knight)
1889–1891

JUNE 14, 1869–MAY 4, 1948

When the widowed Daniel Gould Fowle became governor in 1889, his daughter Helen became his first lady. Helen Fowle, the daughter of Fowle's second wife, Mary Eagles Haywood Fowle, who had died in 1886, was born June 14, 1869, in Raleigh. She attended St. Mary's in the capital city. The year her mother died, Helen Fowle also lost her older brother, Fabius Haywood Fowle, who was killed in a hunting accident at eighteen years of age.

Governor Fowle was inaugurated on January 17, 1889, and he hosted a reception for state leaders following the ceremony. Contemporary newspapers indicate that many friends of the governor's daughter likewise attended the festivities surrounding the inauguration. W. H. Anthony, chief marshal of the reception, presented his regalia to Helen Fowle. Margaret Fowle Andrews, wife of Phillip H. Andrews, and Martha Fowle Avera, wife of David Avera, the governor's two older daughters by his first wife, Ellen Brent Pearson Fowle, attended the ceremony and received guests along with the governor and his younger daughter. Neither of the older daughters lived in Raleigh, inasmuch as they were married and resided elsewhere in North Carolina. The Raleigh *News and Observer* (January 18, 1889) noted that "Miss Helen Fowle, in white plush, silver brocade and diamonds, was the favorite of the ball and was indeed a poem of beauty, grace and loveliness."

Since the Executive Mansion was then unfinished, the Fowles were unable to move into it immediately. They lived in their house on the future site of the Sir Walter Hotel. Since Governor Fowle believed that the residence would never be finished if it remained unoccupied, he and his family moved into the still unfinished mansion on January 5, 1891. They brought with them some of their own furniture to supplement the furnishings the state had provided for its chief executive's residence. The Fowles' new home was uncomfortable, inasmuch as the steam heat had yet to be installed and the plumbing was not completed. Even with the addition of the family's own furniture, the mansion was sparsely furnished. In spite of that situation, on January 13, 1891, the governor and his daughter Helen hosted an elegant opening reception. The *News and Observer* declared the mansion a building of which the state could be proud. Miss Fowle, then only twenty-one years old, with her father and younger siblings Mary Elizabeth and Daniel Gould Jr. became the first family to live in the Executive Mansion, and she became its official hostess. Mary Elizabeth Fowle, who later married Walter M. Stearns, was attending St. Mary's in Raleigh. Daniel Jr. later married Helen Moore and went on to a military career.

Helen Fowle's time in the mansion was brief, as her father died there on April 7, 1891. In spite of her ministrations, Governor Fowle succumbed to heart failure in his second-floor bedroom. The funeral was a sad occasion in Raleigh and for the entire state. The senior class of St. Mary's, students from Wake Forest College, and a host of state dignitaries attended the funeral, which was held at Raleigh's First Presbyterian Church. Once again Miss Fowle's older half sisters helped her carry out her duties as hostess.

Helen Fowle remained in Raleigh, where she married Thomas Duerson Knight on July 22, 1891. The Knights moved to Chicago, Illinois, where he had been appointed assistant state attorney, and they had two sons, one of whom died in infancy. Thomas Duerson, first of the Knights' sons, was born January 21, 1893. Helen Fowle Knight died in Chicago on May 4, 1948, of heart failure. She was buried beside her husband in his family's plot in Cave Hill Cemetery in Louisville, Kentucky.

Louisa Matilda Moore Holt

1891–1893

OCTOBER 15, 1833–DECEMBER 9, 1899

Upon the unexpected death of Governor Daniel G. Fowle, Lieutenant Governor Thomas Michael Holt assumed the governorship of North Carolina. Because of a recent bereavement in the family, Mrs. Holt did not often go to Raleigh while her husband was governor.

Louisa Matilda Moore was born in Caswell County on October 15, 1833, to prosperous planter Samuel Moore and his wife Mary A. Bethel Moore. The young woman and the wealthy Thomas M. Holt of Alamance County were married on October 17, 1855, at her home, Mount Pleasant. They lived at Linwood, the Holt plantation in Davidson County. They later moved to an estate in Haw River, where he owned textile mills and built a spacious home. The house, which stood on the west bank of the Haw River, was large and ornate, with many conveniences. It contained seven bedrooms and two baths and included a connected kitchen and numerous outbuildings. Thomas Holt made a conscious effort to plant trees of all varieties, so long as they were native to North Carolina, on the more than four-hundred-acre estate. A spacious lawn, orchards, and vegetable gardens on nine acres surrounded the house, making it a local showplace.

The Holts had six children. Alice Linwood Holt was born in 1856 and died the following year. Charles Thomas Holt was born January 9, 1858, and later married Gena Jones, daughter of the governor of Alabama; they had one daughter. Cora May Holt was born December 17, 1859, and was later wed to Dr. Edward Chambers Laird; they had two sons. Louisa Moore, called "Daisy," was born March 16, 1861. She later married Alfred Williams Haywood of

Governor and Mrs. Holt's home in Haw River

Raleigh and had two sons. Ella Moore Holt was born December 7, 1862, and later married Charles Bruce Wright; the union produced two sons. The youngest of the Holts' sons was Thomas Michael Jr., who was born September 11, 1871, and died in 1897.

The Holt family, like most of the wealthy elite of their time, visited the fashionable resorts of the day. Buffalo Lithia Springs in Mecklenburg County, Virginia, was a favorite destination. There guests spent their mornings playing cards, bowling, or reading. Because of the governor's health (he had Bright's disease), he and his wife often visited Philadelphia for treatment and sometimes went to Florida for rest.

Louisa Holt was known as a personable, kind, and intelligent woman whose husband was very devoted to and protective of her. She had a tranquil goodness that endeared her to those who came to visit. Mrs. Holt was also shy, which may explain her uneasiness in performing the duties expected of the first lady. The Holts' daughter Daisy Haywood, who resided in Raleigh only two blocks away from the Executive Mansion, was more outgoing than her mother and often acted as official hostess for her father. In the early 1890s the mansion still had very little furniture. An article about the mansion that appeared in the Raleigh *News and Observer* in 1938 reported that Mrs. Haywood "decided that the simplest solution would be to move her 10-room household, complete with servants, to the Executive Mansion." The governor himself brought to the mansion some of his own furniture from his permanent home in Haw River.

Louisa Moore Holt died suddenly of heart failure on December 9, 1899. She was visiting her sister in Burlington for a few days at the time of her death. Following a simple funeral service at the Presbyterian church in Graham, she was buried in Linwood Cemetery in Graham, North Carolina, beside her husband and several of their children.

William Eleanor Kearny Carr
1893–1897

MARCH 1, 1840–MARCH 29, 1912

Eleanor Kearny, the daughter of wealthy Warren County planter William Kinchen Kearny and his wife Benjamin Hardee James Maria Alston, was born on March 1, 1840. She was well educated by private tutors and at a girls' school in Petersburg, Virginia. She married wealthy planter Elias Carr on May 24, 1859. The wedding was a social event in Warren County, and a lavish reception followed. Carr, a well-to-do country gentleman, gave his wife an elaborate wedding ring—an opal surrounded by diamonds.

The Carrs lived at his residence, Bracebridge Hall, in Edgecombe County. Because Eleanor's father was convinced that the air there was more conducive to the spread of malaria, she promised him that she would not spend summers at her new home but would return to the healthier Warren County. During the early years of her marriage, she and the children spent the summers at Huntersville, her family home in Warren County. In 1867 Carr purchased a Warrenton estate for his wife so that she might spend her summers in the more favorable climate. While he remained at Bracebridge Hall to manage the plantation during the summer months, he wrote numerous letters to Eleanor in Warrenton. The letters indicate how badly he missed her and the children and how much he looked forward to being together again. In addition to expressing such tender feelings, Carr's letters often discussed politics with his wife. He related news of the plantation and kept her abreast of events in the area.

The Carrs had six children. William Kearny was born in 1860, John Buxton in 1862, Mary Elizabeth in 1864 (she died in 1866), Elias Jr. in 1866, Eleanor Kearny in 1881, and Annie Bruce in 1884. William later married Martina Van Riswick, Elias Jr. married Maud Montgomery Inge, Eleanor was wed to Hugh Matthews, and Annie married Douglas Sterrett.

Mrs. Carr, a retiring woman by nature, was somewhat uncomfortable in her role as hostess at the Executive Mansion. Her daughter-in-law, Martina Van Riswick Carr, wife of her son William, assisted her and proved to be an asset, inasmuch as she enjoyed society. In February 1893 the legislature allocated funds to purchase furniture for and to complete and repair the mansion. Much work was done on the house and grounds during Elias Carr's administration. It was during those years that David Haywood, whom members of numerous first families called "Uncle Dave," came to the mansion as butler. Haywood's devotion to the first family was unerring, and he served fourteen governors' families during his long career.

Mrs. Carr in her inaugural ball gown

Both the Carrs were interested in genealogy and were charter members of two North Carolina ancestral societies—Elias of the Sons and Eleanor of the Daughters of the Revolution. He was the first president of his society; she was the first librarian of hers. Mrs. Carr was reared as a Methodist but joined the Episcopalian faith after her marriage. Throughout her life, however, she continued to attend services in churches of both denominations. She made certain that her children received religious instruction in their home. Her concern extended to their intellectual well-being as well. All received private educations both at home and in various schools. In spite of her wealthy upbringing, Eleanor Carr ran the household at Bracebridge Hall very efficiently, doing much of the cooking and sewing herself.

Governor and Mrs. Carr (both seated) and daughter Annie Bruce on front porch of their home, Bracebridge Hall, in Edgecombe County

Eleanor Kearny Carr died on March 29, 1912, in Washington, D.C., where she had gone to undergo surgery and was staying with her son. Her body was returned to North Carolina and buried at Bracebridge Hall.

Sarah Amanda Sanders Russell

1897–1901

AUGUST 31, 1844–MARCH 18, 1913

Republican governor Daniel Lindsay Russell took office in January 1897 with wife Amanda by his side. In an age and area in which support for the emancipation of slaves and an acceptance of African Americans as political equals were not popular, Daniel Russell alienated southern Democrats. With genuine concern for the betterment of society, he pushed for reforms, especially regulation of railroads, and that stance alienated the pro-business segment of his own Republican Party. Moreover, in 1898 and again in 1900, North Carolina's Democrats mounted a white-supremacy campaign that often became violent. The governor was concerned about how the challenges he faced might affect his wife, who, he said, "was a quiet person well-known for her activities in the temperance cause." Mrs. Russell, a strong woman who was just as concerned for her husband as he was for her, remained steadfast throughout his controversial term.

Even as Amanda Sanders, daughter of Onslow County's Colonel Isaac Newton Sanders and his wife, Caroline Burns Sanders, Mrs. Russell was no stranger to controversy. When the Civil War began, her father refused to participate on either side because he opposed secession and the war. Because supporters of the Confederacy and the Union alike considered him a traitor, he spent much of his time in hiding. While Governor John W. Ellis had stripped Sanders of his militia rank as colonel, Governor Zebulon B. Vance, Ellis's successor, commissioned him captain of the Home Defense, thus enabling Sanders to come out of hiding.

Amanda Sanders, educated in Beaufort and later at St. Mary's in Raleigh, maintained a lifelong love of literature. When her father died in 1866 she and her younger sister Alice went to live with their uncle, John Sanders, at his Onslow County home, Elm Grove. There, on August 16, 1869, Miss Sanders married her cousin, Daniel Russell, whose family was quite wealthy. The newlyweds immediately faced the possibility of violence, inasmuch as the political climate of Reconstruction was unfavorable to Republicans. Russell had moved to Wilmington and been elected a judge of the superior court. He faced so many threats of physical violence that he was obliged to purchase a house closer to the courthouse. His widowed grandmother Alice Mitchell Sanders, who had reared him, lived with the young couple until she died in 1881. Following a later term in Congress and a temporary move to Washington, D.C., the Russells moved back to Wilmington, where Daniel practiced law. Later they lived at Belleville, their plantation in Brunswick County. The plantation produced rice and turpentine. During that time Amanda Russell started a dairy that came to be one of her lifelong interests. The kind and gracious woman began to share her good fortune with others in her community, often giving milk to people who had none.

A strong interest in the care of family members was another facet of the Russells' life together. Throughout their lives, numerous family members came to live with them. Although they had no children of their own, they enjoyed the company of many nieces and nephews, grandnieces and grandnephews, who lived with them. Indeed, even after the Russells moved into the Executive Mansion, one niece lived with them for the entire four years, and two others were there much of the time. A grandnephew named Daniel Russell Sawyer was born there on December 31, 1897.

Remembrances by Amanda Russell's grandniece indicate how independent and strong this first lady was, as well as how influential she was on her younger relatives. According to her grandniece Alice Sawyer Cooper, "Mrs. Russell was herself a strong-minded, intelligent woman with a lively sense of humor, a quiet but deep religious belief . . . " (Jeffrey J. Crow and Robert F. Durden, *Maverick Republican in the Old North State: A Political Biography of Daniel L. Russell*, 12).

Amanda Russell died March 18, 1913, following an illness of several months. Her obituary stated that she "was remarkably gifted in personal attraction and mental qualities. While the first lady of the State at the Executive Mansion, Mrs. Russell took a firm stand for temperance. Her courage and independence did much to make the movement a popular one a few years later" (Raleigh *News and Observer*, March 19, 1913). Amanda Russell likewise held strong opinions concerning the Executive Mansion, especially the kitchen, which was then downstairs and had no window. When the legislature appropriated funds, she had the kitchen moved upstairs, where conditions were much brighter. Amanda Russell was buried in the Aman Cemetery in Onslow County.

Cora Lily Woodard Aycock

1901–1905

OCTOBER 11, 1868–MARCH 13, 1952

Just as first ladies before her had discovered, Cora Aycock in 1901 found that the governor's annual salary of three thousand dollars was inadequate to cover frivolous or elaborate entertaining at the Executive Mansion; and just as former first ladies had managed, so too did Mrs. Aycock. (Indeed, the family, being of modest means, left office in debt, in part because of personal expenses associated with being governor.) Mrs. Aycock skillfully hosted the small dinners for friends and colleagues that her husband, Governor Charles Brantley Aycock, preferred. Both of them relished simple entertaining and did not undertake many large events at the mansion. Many children were entertained there, however, as the Aycocks' many children often invited their friends to visit. Cora Aycock also encouraged her husband's interest in education and in her later years saw the fruits of his labors ripen as he was accorded the title of North Carolina's education governor.

Cora Lily Woodard was the second wife of Charles B. Aycock. They were married on January 7, 1891. Her older sister, Varina, Aycock's first wife, died July 9, 1889, following eight years of marriage. With his first wife, Aycock had three children. Ernest Aycock was born in 1882 and died as an infant. Charles Brantley Aycock Jr. was born December 28, 1883, and died of spinal meningitis on August 10, 1901, while his father was governor. Alice Varina Aycock was born in 1886 and later married Clarence Poe. Varina Aycock's children loved Cora Aycock and were reared with Cora's own children. William Benjamin Aycock was born March 23, 1892, and later married Lucile Best; Mary Lily Aycock was born October 1, 1893, and later married Lennox Polk McLendon; Connor Woodard Aycock was born

Mrs. Aycock in inaugural ball gown by Worth of Paris

November 14, 1895; and John Lee Aycock was born August 7, 1897. Louise Rountree Aycock was born September 4, 1899; Frank Daniels Aycock was born July 9, 1902, in the mansion; and Brantley (who subsequently changed his name to Charles Brantley) Aycock was born August 12, 1907, and later married Alice Brogden. While in the Executive Mansion, Cora Aycock gave most of her attention to rearing her children and her duties as first lady. She was also active in her church, maintaining her membership in the Primitive Baptist church in Wilson. This musical woman played the piano beautifully and instilled in her children an appreciation for music. Their home was often filled with the sound of it.

After the Aycocks left office, they moved back to Goldsboro, where they had resided before moving to Raleigh. In 1910 the family moved back to Raleigh. Charles B. Aycock died suddenly on April 4, 1912, while delivering an address before the Alabama Education Association in Birmingham. Left with almost no estate and eight children, the spunky former first lady took matters in hand. At their Raleigh home, located on a one-acre tract, she raised a variety of vegetables and kept chickens and a cow. She taught her children to be thrifty and allowed them to sell any extra milk or vegetables. She inherited from her parents a farm in Wilson County adjacent to that of a brother-in-law, who oversaw its operation. From that farm her family received a modest income from the sale of tobacco and was provided ham and sausage. Cora Aycock helped to support her family by publishing and selling *The Life and Speeches of Charles B. Aycock*, which was edited by historian R. D. W. Connor and her son-in-law Clarence Poe. Later in her life, Mrs. Aycock, never very interested in politics, was appointed president of the North Carolina Railroad Company by then governor J. C. B. Ehringhaus.

Born October 11, 1868, to Elder William and Delpha Rountree Woodard of Wilson, Cora Woodard Aycock was the daughter of a Primitive Baptist lay preacher and farmer. She was educated at Wilson Collegiate Institute and attended Mary Baldwin College in Staunton, Virginia. Following a long illness, Cora Aycock died on March 13, 1952, and was buried beside her husband in Raleigh's Oakwood Cemetery.

Cornelia G. "Nina" Deaderick Glenn

1905–1909

SEPTEMBER 4, 1854–DECEMBER 9, 1926

Cornelia G. "Nina" Glenn, wife of Governor Robert Brodnax Glenn, introduced caterers and an air of formality to the Executive Mansion. Servants there served all meals, including breakfast, with full silver place settings in a formal atmosphere. Mrs. Glenn's parties were lavish and well planned. Among a number of dignitaries who visited the mansion during her husband's term of office were William Jennings Bryan and President William Howard Taft. Like first ladies before her, Nina Glenn graciously presided over many luncheons and teas, in spite of her innate shyness. She was very proper and firmly backed her husband's championship of statewide prohibition. Her own interests included gardening and music. Residing in the Executive Mansion along with the Glenns (except for their son Chalmers, who was married and lived elsewhere) was Ann Dodge Glenn, called Dodge, a niece of the governor, who recalled that Mrs. Glenn could be quite stern but entertained beautifully.

In its coverage of Robert B. Glenn's inauguration as governor and related festivities, the Raleigh *News and Observer* commented on the large party of Winston-Salem citizens that accompanied the Glenns to Raleigh. Not only the Glenns' family but also many of their friends attended the events of January 6, 12, and 13, 1905. The reception was not held at the Executive Mansion, as had been customary, nor, after the inauguration, were the Glenns able to move into the mansion because it was under quarantine. Louise Aycock, daughter of Governor Glenn's predecessor, had diphtheria and, with Mrs. Aycock, remained in the mansion. It was not until January 17 that the Aycocks, the doctor, and the nurse who helped care for the child were able to leave and the Glenns could move into their new official home.

Nina Glenn with son Chalmers and daughter Rebekah

Nina Glenn with grandson Chalmers

Nina Deaderick, born September 4, 1854, in Jonesboro, Tennessee, to John Franklin and Rebecca Lanier Williams Deaderick, was the youngest of a large number of children. The Deadericks were a prominent, civic-minded Tennessee family. One of Nina Deaderick's uncles was the chief justice of the Tennessee Supreme Court. Another of her uncles was a United States senator from Tennessee, and still another was a member of that state's General Assembly. Her grandfather, David Deaderick, likewise served in the Tennessee General Assembly and was a prominent businessman.

On January 8, 1878, Nina married Robert Glenn in Knoxville, Tennessee. Glenn and his new wife were actually distant cousins through their mothers. Rebecca L. Williams Deaderick's sister, Susan, married James R. Dodge. Their daughter, Annie Dodge, married Chalmers L. Glenn, father of Robert Brodnax Glenn. Robert and Nina Glenn had two sons and a daughter. Chalmers Lanier Glenn was born January 5, 1879, and later married Jessie Morrow and had one son. Frank was born in 1880 and died the following year. Rebekah Williams Glenn was born April 28, 1883, and later married Daniel E. Hoffman and had two daughters. In 1885 the Glenns moved to Winston-Salem from Stokes County, where Robert Glenn had practiced law and which he had represented in the state legislature.

After the Glenns left Raleigh they moved back to Winston-Salem, where Mrs. Glenn was active in the First Presbyterian Church. Her obituary in the Winston-Salem *Journal* (December 10, 1926) quoted her friend, Mrs. W. C. Wright: "'She adhered to the simple tastes of life—her home, family, church and friends were the center of her heart's desire and sacred interest.'" An editorial in the same issue declared: "Always she insisted with unostentatious firmness upon being faithful to the principles which she deemed to be necessary to right living."

Nina Deaderick Glenn died of a lengthy illness on December 9, 1926, at the age of seventy-two. She was buried in Salem Cemetery in Winston-Salem.

Sue Musette Satterfield Kitchin

1909–1913

MARCH 10, 1874–NOVEMBER 4, 1956

Charming and charismatic, Musette Kitchin, wife of Governor William Walton Kitchin, was comfortable with the entertaining necessary to a governor's wife. During her husband's administration, the Executive Mansion was often full of family and friends and was the residence of a large number of people. In addition to the family of seven, two of Mrs. Kitchin's sisters lived with them, and, during one winter, two of Governor Kitchin's brothers did likewise. Mrs. Kitchin also hosted "at home" days during which many people visited the mansion. As an obituary in the *Scotland Neck Commonwealth* (November 9, 1956) declared, she will be remembered "for her personal charm, friendliness, and quality of character. . . ." An editorial in the same issue noted that she "graced the Executive Mansion and charmed all who visited. But she never let this great prestige affect her outlook on life or her attitude toward others." She had an innate ability to remember names and always made people feel at ease by calling their name whenever she met them.

In spite of a decline in her husband's income (the governor's salary was $4,000 plus $500 for entertaining, and William Kitchin had earned more than $7,500 as a congressman), Musette Kitchin hosted numerous parties and stayed within the budget. Because the governor ran on a platform of cutting the budget, no renovations or redecoration occurred during his tenure in the Executive Mansion. In a much later newspaper article (Raleigh *News and Observer*, February 6, 1938), Mrs. Kitchin commented on the plain (even ugly in spots) comfort of the house while she and her husband had resided there. She did, however, purchase a piano and some flat silver for the mansion.

Born in Roxboro to William Clement Satterfield and Sue Temesia Norwood Satterfield on March 10, 1874, Sue Musette Satterfield graduated from Greensboro Female College (now Greensboro College) in 1891 and married William Walton Kitchin on December 22, 1892. They had six children: Sue Arrington was born October 22, 1893, and later married William Thomas Joyner; William Walton Jr. was born in 1895 and died when he was ten years old; Anne Maria was born October 23, 1897, and later married Edward Llewellyn Travis; Elizabeth Gertrude was born December 19, 1899, and subsequently married Germaine Simpson Brown; Clement Satterfield was born June 19, 1902, and never married; and Musette Satterfield was born August 10, 1906, and later married Sam Arrington Dunn Jr.

Mrs. Kitchin was concerned about the education of her children and took them to opera performances. It was important to her that the children learned to appreciate music. She also took time at night to read Bible stories to them and give each one some personal attention. Even though Mrs. Kitchin was a Methodist and the governor was a Baptist, the family alternated between churches of both faiths, and each child eventually made his or her own decision about which denomination to choose.

Kitchin family portrait. From left, first row—Governor Kitchin (seated), holding Clement Satterfield; Musette Satterfield (seated); Mrs. Kitchin (seated); second row—Anne Maria, Elizabeth Gertrude; third row—Sue Arrington

In Scotland Neck, their hometown, Musette Kitchin belonged to numerous civic organizations. She was also active in the Scotland Neck Methodist Church, where she served on the board of stewards, and was a director of the Methodist Orphanage. At the end of Governor Kitchin's term in office, the family remained in Raleigh as he entered a law practice with Judge James S. Manning. William Kitchin suffered a stroke in 1919, and the family retired to Scotland Neck. Mrs. Kitchin resumed her social and civic activities in that town and again became involved in church activities.

Musette Satterfield Kitchin died November 4, 1956, of a brief illness after suffering a heart attack. She died in the hospital in Tarboro and was buried in the Baptist Cemetery in Scotland Neck.

Annie D. M. Burgin Craig

1913–1917

MARCH 15, 1873–NOVEMBER 6, 1955

Following their marriage on November 18, 1891, in McDowell County, Locke and Annie Burgin Craig lived in Asheville, where three of their four sons were born. It was there that Locke Craig enjoyed a successful law practice. Rearing their sons with good humor and fun, Annie Craig enjoyed her children, encouraged their interest in sports, and entertained their friends. She also enjoyed the entertaining that was expected of her when she moved into the Executive Mansion. She brought her innate good nature to that task as well. A personable woman, Mrs. Craig was liked by everyone she met. She was a good listener and knew how to make people feel at ease. As was always the case, Raleigh provided lavish entertainments for Locke Craig's inauguration. Numerous friends and family from western North Carolina accompanied the Craigs to the capital city. Mrs. Josephus Daniels hosted a luncheon for Annie Craig and her guests to introduce her to Raleigh and the wives of members of the General Assembly.

Annie Burgin, born in Old Fort, McDowell County, to Captain Joseph B. and Margaret E. Burgin Burgin on March 15, 1873, was one of four children. She had two brothers and one sister. Although both of her parents shared the surname Burgin, they were not, or were only very distantly, related to one another.

The Craigs had four sons. The oldest three were born in Asheville, and the youngest, Locke Jr., was born November 11, 1914, in the Executive Mansion; he later married and had three daughters. Carlyle Craig was born October 30, 1892; George Winston Craig was born June 18, 1894, and later married Mary Kathryne Taylor and had two daughters; and Arthur

Burgin was born March 11, 1896, and later married and had two daughters and a son. Two of the Craigs' sons were educated for the military and graduated from the U.S. Naval Academy at Annapolis. Carlyle saw active duty in World War II, Arthur later went to work for an airline, and Locke Jr. became a forester.

Annie Craig was devoted to her sons. In an interview, her son George, who subsequently served as a member of the North Carolina General Assembly and practiced law in Asheville, recounted the time that his mother nursed him back to health in the Executive Mansion. He suffered for fourteen weeks with typhoid fever. Later, after they had moved back to Asheville, she nursed her husband, who was an invalid for seven years before he died in 1924. Her family was very important to her, and she was willing to make many sacrifices for them.

Mrs. Craig in later years, after serving as first lady

After their time at the mansion the Craigs moved back to Asheville, where they built a new house on their property on the Swannanoa River. There Mrs. Craig was able to resume her life with friends and family. Annie Craig enjoyed playing bridge and, from all reports, was a skilled and competitive player. She played the game with friends until she moved into a nursing home the year before she died. A member of First Presbyterian Church, the Current Literature Club, and other organizations, Mrs. Craig was a genuine lover of people. All who met her were drawn to the charming, caring woman.

Mrs. Craig died in Asheville on November 6, 1955. About six weeks before she died she suffered a stroke from which she never recovered. Annie Burgin Craig was buried beside her husband in Riverside Cemetery in Asheville.

Fanny Neal Yarborough Bickett

1917–1921

OCTOBER 11, 1870–JULY 2, 1941

Fanny Yarborough Bickett was the first of the first ladies to have a profession outside of the home. She was also among the most formally educated. Mrs. Bickett had long been active in social work before her husband became governor, and she continued actively in that profession until her death in 1941. She was a pioneer in the days before public assistance and through her lobbying efforts and political influence was instrumental in the development of the welfare system in North Carolina. Governor Thomas Walter Bickett was interested in the welfare of his constituents as well, perhaps to the credit of his wife. During his administration many social reforms, including establishment of juvenile courts, stricter regulations regarding hiring of minors, better treatment of prisoners, and increased public health services, were implemented.

Fanny Yarborough was born October 11, 1870, at Rose Hill, the family home in Franklin County. Her mother, Lucy (Lula) Massenburg Davis Yarborough, died when she was only three. Her father, Colonel William Henry Yarborough (CSA), and an aunt, Fannie Yarborough Neal, of Louisburg, reared her. First educated by a private governess, then at Louisburg College, she graduated from St. Mary's in Raleigh in 1889. She then studied for two years at the University of Chicago and took special work at Harvard University. At various times, she studied at the University of North Carolina in Chapel Hill. Following her husband's death, she attended law school at Wake Forest College and eventually passed the North Carolina State Bar, receiving a license to practice law at the age of sixty.

Mrs. Bickett in mansion vegetable garden

Early in the Bickett administration, architect James Salter conducted a complete inspection of the Executive Mansion. Mrs. Bickett supported Salter's suggestions to improve the building and forwarded them to the General Assembly's Joint Committee on Public Buildings and Grounds. Salter's original estimate of $65,000 failed to pass the General Assembly; but a substitute measure enacted in March 1917 granted $4,000 for the project, and a subsequent allocation in 1919 gained another $4,000 for continued refurbishment. In 1920 the second-floor ballroom was converted into a bedroom, bath, closets, and a corridor that connected other family bedrooms. Mrs. Bickett purchased dining-room furniture, a four-poster bed for the guest room, and the elaborate console table with mirror in the Grand Hallway.

When the Bicketts moved into the mansion, Mrs. Bickett brought along her own household staff from Louisburg, including Nancy, the family cook. Family members said that cooking was not among Mrs. Bickett's many talents; some doubted that she could turn on the stove. Nancy did all the cooking while the Bicketts occupied the mansion. During World War I Fanny Bickett promoted home gardens across the state to aid in the war effort. Those efforts included her own victory garden at the Executive Mansion. In 1918 the first lady went to France to visit American troops as a representative of the YMCA. Throughout the war Mrs. Bickett provided housing in the Executive Mansion for soldiers passing through Raleigh. As many as sixty cots remained set up in the second-floor Ballroom to provide a place of rest for those men. In 1920 Fanny Bickett and her husband, along with suffrage leaders, appeared before a joint session of the legislature in support of women's suffrage.

Less than a year after completing his term as governor, Thomas Walter Bickett died on December 28, 1921. Soon thereafter, Mrs. Bickett became head of the Infant and Maternal Welfare Bureau of the State Department of Health. She served in that capacity until 1924, when she became the superintendent of public welfare for Wake County. At that time, little or no money was funneled into welfare programs, and she had to depend on her own ingenuity to aid as many people as possible.

In 1937 the North Carolina General Assembly enacted two laws relating to the federal Social Security Act of 1935; the laws dealt with how public welfare was to be administered in the state. A burgeoning program developed. Mrs. Bickett's office grew from herself and one secretary to twenty-four people. Known for her evenhanded racial policy, Mrs. Bickett hired several African Americans for both professional and clerical positions in the office. She was known as well for her effective handling of cases and staff and for her unyielding professionalism. Helping people was Mrs. Bickett's first love, and she felt much compassion for her clients on the welfare rolls.

In 1929 Governor O. Max Gardner appointed Fanny Bickett president of the North Carolina Railroad Company; she was the first woman to serve in that post, which carried with it an annual salary of twelve hundred dollars and entitled her to free railroad travel throughout the nation. The duties were largely ceremonial and involved attending two meetings of the board of directors each year. Mrs. Bickett was also a member of the board of the North Carolina School for the Blind and was instrumental in developing the juvenile court system in Wake County. She worked with the U.S. Training Corps, an organization established by the War Department in 1918 to improve the physical condition of women working in offices and in war-related capacities. She was commandant of the Southeastern District of the Training Corps, serving several summers at a camp near Asheville. She was a national officer in the Colonial Dames of America and was also an active member of the United Daughters of the Confederacy

Governor and Mrs. Bickett with son William Yarborough

and the Daughters of the American Revolution. Mrs. Bickett was actively involved in the YMCA and YWCA, especially during World War I. A lifelong Episcopalian, she was also involved with the work of Christ Church in Raleigh.

Thomas Walter Bickett and Fanny Neal Yarborough were married on November 29, 1898, in Franklin County. They met in Louisburg, seat of Franklin County, where Mr. Bickett was a young country lawyer. She was from a prominent, well-to-do Franklin County family, and Mr. Bickett was from Monroe, where his father was a physician. His mother was Mary Covington Bickett, sister of United States senator David Covington. Thomas Bickett graduated from Wake Forest College and taught school in Winston-Salem, then practiced law in Stokes County for a brief time before relocating his practice to Louisburg. The Bicketts had three children, but only one, a son, William Yarborough Bickett, born August 30, 1899, survived infancy. A second son, Thomas Walter Jr., was born October 7, 1901, and died in 1902. A daughter, Mary Covington, was born June 8, 1903, and died in 1904. The loss of two children affected Mrs. Bickett for the rest of her life and perhaps guided her interest in child welfare.

Mrs. Bickett (first row, seventh from right) with group of women in front of mansion

William Yarborough Bickett, a superior court judge, and his family lived with Fanny Bickett during the last twenty years of her life. In her later years, Mrs. Bickett took up the hobby of knitting for relaxation. She dabbled in oils and crayon and especially loved painting mountain scenes. She never slept well and, being an avid reader, often took four or five books to bed with her, reading half of them before morning. Among her personal pleasures was enjoying the company of her grandchildren, William's three daughters Frances Yarborough, Cecile Meetze, and Caroline Pinckney.

Fanny Yarborough Bickett died at Rex Hospital in Raleigh on July 2, 1941, following a heart attack. Her funeral was held at her beloved Christ Episcopal Church, where her passing was mourned by the entire city of Raleigh. She was buried beside Governor Bickett at Oak Lawn Memorial Cemetery in Louisburg.

Angelia Lawrance Morrison (Harris)
1921–1925

MARCH 24, 1912–JULY 13, 1983

Having lost her mother, Lottie May Tomlinson Morrison, in 1919, Angelia Lawrance Morrison excitedly accepted the role of "little mistress of the mansion" when her father, Governor Cameron Morrison, was inaugurated on January 12, 1921. Accompanying her father and his sisters Ida Morrison and Ada Morrison Nuttall, as well as three hundred residents of Charlotte, on a train to Raleigh, Angelia was the center of attention. By all accounts she was at her father's side during all of the day's events, from breakfast aboard the train to the ball that evening.

Upon her initial arrival at the Executive Mansion, Angelia Morrison emerged from a limousine along with her father, surveyed the outgoing Governor and Mrs. Bickett, then ran up the stairs, meeting the first lady with open arms, and proceeded to hug and kiss her and then the governor. Attired in brown velvet dress, coat and hat with matching kid gloves, and a corsage of sweet peas and lilies of the valley, Miss Morrison proceeded into the city auditorium on the arms of both her father and Governor Bickett. Following the inaugural ceremony, a group of ladies from Charlotte presented a large bouquet of American Beauty roses to Governor Morrison, who then handed them to Angelia.

The Morrisons returned to the Executive Mansion for luncheon with the immediate family. Dinner that evening had been prepared and left ready by Mrs. Bickett, who had also readied the rest of the mansion for the incoming family—even to decorating a room especially for the eight-year-old first lady. From 8:30 to 10:30 P.M. there were receptions at the Executive Mansion and at the Woman's Club of Raleigh, and at both Angelia Morrison stood proudly

Angelia with her father, Governor Morrison, at his inauguration

next to her father shaking hands with well-wishers. She was dressed, according to the *Charlotte Observer* of January 14, 1921, in "an exquisite frock of soft white silk and lace with her hair tied with a big white satin bow and slippers and stockings of white. She wore a corsage of white rosebuds and lilies of the valley." The newspaper further described the child as "resplendent almost in every detail. On the car, on the stage, at lunch, in the receiving line at the ball last night, she was almost the central figure. The state likes Angelia and it welcomed her with courtesies probably exceeding any ever accorded a child of Carolina."

Governor Morrison continued to keep his only child involved in his active life, allowing her to accompany him as often as possible. Angelia traveled with her father throughout the state and participated in a variety of activities expected of a first lady. Whenever he traveled outside the state, the governor always brought Angelia presents, particularly clothing in his favorite color, red. Cameron and Angelia Morrison's fondness for one another continued throughout his lifetime.

When Governor Morrison married Mrs. Sara Virginia Ecker Watts on April 2, 1924, he took his daughter and his sister Ida, along with distinguished members of his administration, to witness the ceremony. Until this second marriage, Angelia and one of the governor's sisters, Ida Morrison, performed the duties of first lady. Also residing at the Executive Mansion during Cameron Morrison's tenure were his secretary, Margaret Willis, and at times his widowed sister, Ada Morrison Nuttall. The new Mrs. Morrison commissioned a portrait of Angelia's mother as a present for the child so that she would have her mother ever present in her life. At the end of her father's term in office, Angelia Morrison left the mansion with her aunt Ida Morrison and returned to the family's Charlotte home prior to her father and stepmother's arrival. Later in life Angelia Morrison inherited Morrocroft, the English manor her father and stepmother built.

ngelia christening Carr E. Booker's airplane

Angelia Morrison graduated from Spence School in New York and attended Sweet Briar College. Her daughter Sara has described her as having loved people and having never met a stranger. In October 1932 Angelia married James Jackson Harris and reared four children—James Jackson Harris Jr., born May 2, 1936 (died 1990); Sara Harris, born May 25, 1938 (married Howard Cary Bissell on May 21, 1960); Cameron Morrison Harris, born December 14, 1943 (married Dorothy Waller on September 6, 1969); and John William Harris, born July 3, 1947 (married Deborah Small on April 25, 1970). She named her only daughter after her beloved stepmother, Sara Ecker Watts Morrison.

In 1964 Angelia Morrison Harris opened and actively operated a successful antiques business in Charlotte. In 1967, at the behest of his wife, Governor Dan K. Moore appointed her to serve as a member of the Executive Mansion Fine Arts Commission. Mrs. Harris's infectious spontaneity had a joyous effect on that body's activities. She and generous fellow member Ralph Hanes engaged in uproarious discussions on the pros and cons of Victorian furniture. The committee enjoyed the fun of working with her and gained knowledge from her expertise.

Mrs. Harris was also involved in many organizations, among them the Charlotte Debutante Club and Covenant Presbyterian Church. She was a benefactor to Queens College, St. Andrews Presbyterian College, the Mint Museum, and Charlotte Country Day School. Angelia Morrison Harris died on July 13, 1983, at the age of seventy-one.

Angelia with her father, Governor Morrison, beginning a trip from the State Capitol

Sara Virginia Ecker Watts Morrison

1924–1925

MARCH 14, 1868–MAY 26, 1950

Governor Cameron Morrison surprised most people when he married Mrs. Sara Virginia Ecker Watts on April 2, 1924, at Harwood Hall in Durham. The governor had been a widower since 1919, the year his first wife, Lottie May Tomlinson Morrison, died. Following the newly married couple's honeymoon in New York, they returned to the Executive Mansion.

Mrs. Morrison was born March 14, 1868, in Belle Isle, New York, to Isaac Scott and Mary Scott Ecker. She had at least two sisters and a brother. While growing up, she developed a deep awareness of the individual's role in a "Divine Plan," which gave her a feeling of responsibility for others. Her chosen education and profession were directly tied to her beliefs. She received a nursing degree from Johns Hopkins University and was employed there.

While at Johns Hopkins Hospital she met her first husband, George Washington Watts, who was attending to his wife, who was ill. Sara Ecker served as a private-duty nurse in Durham until Mrs. Watts's death in 1916. George W. Watts and Sara Ecker were married in 1917 and lived at Harwood Hall, their residence in Durham, until his death in 1921. Sara Watts inherited considerable wealth from her husband and continued the philanthropy he had practiced.

Sara Morrison's personality served her well during her short tenure as first lady. She was friendly and warm and made visitors feel at home and comfortable. Not having grown up with elaborate entertaining, she became accustomed to that life-style while married to her first husband. Having been a professional woman and single for much of her adult life, she developed level-headedness and a sense of what she wanted. She employed her management skills and sense of caring to her new vocation as first lady.

Upon leaving the Executive Mansion, Governor and Mrs. Morrison remained for a time at Harwood Hall in Durham before continuing to the governor's own home in Charlotte. His daughter Angelia and sister Ida Morrison went immediately to Charlotte. Soon afterward the couple built a new home and farm known as Morrocroft. When Governor O. Max Gardner appointed Cameron Morrison to a vacant seat in the United States Senate, the couple moved to Washington, D.C. After Morrison lost a bid for election to a full term in the Senate, he and his wife moved back to their beloved home and farm in Charlotte.

Governor and Mrs. Morrison at the time of their marriage

Mrs. Morrison enjoyed needlework; gardening and reading were likewise hobbies. She helped operate the Welcome Wagon service in Charlotte. She and her husband assisted hundreds of young men and women in their quest to receive a higher education. They were concerned for the well-being and comfort of the tenants on their farm and home, as well as the education of the tenants' children. Of great importance to Sara Morrison were the Presbyterian Church, local and worldwide mission work, and educational endeavors. She always shied away from publicity and often did her kind deeds anonymously. The chapel at Convenant Presbyterian Church is named for her, as is a building at Queens College. In 1930 Davidson College presented her with the Algernon Sydney Sullivan Award for service to humanity. She endowed the Assembly Training School and the Union Theological Seminary in Richmond, as well as the Stuart Robinson School in Blackey, Kentucky. She was a member of the board of trustees for Stonewall Jackson Training School in Concord, the YWCA in Durham and Charlotte, Queens College in Charlotte, and Watts Hospital in Durham.

Preceding her husband in death, Sara Morrison passed away on May 26, 1950, from cancer and was buried at Charlotte's Elmwood Cemetery. At the time of her death, an editorial in the *Charlotte News* (May 27, 1950) pointed out that "Wealthy people differ in their attitudes towards their possessions. Mrs. Cameron Morrison belonged to the group of wealthy individuals who feel that their good fortune gives them an opportunity to put some of their wealth to use for the benefit of the community and society in general. Quietly, unostentatiously she managed to strike a nice balance in her dual role as wife of an important public servant and benefactress of many worthy institutions and undertakings. . . . [H]er influence went far beyond the circle of her personal friends and acquaintances and will last for a long time."

Margaret Jones French McLean

1925–1929

APRIL 29, 1879 – NOVEMBER 1, 1959

Having become a savvy entertainer and hostess at home in Lumberton, Margaret Jones French McLean was at ease and enjoyed the opportunities presented to her while first lady. She was accustomed to large gatherings of family, friends, and business and political associates of her husband. The McLeans were prominent and prosperous residents of a small rural town, and there had been many opportunities for Mrs. McLean to offer her creative hospitality to a variety of guests. To her disappointment, however, she was unable to attend the most elaborate inaugural events inasmuch as she was afflicted with pneumonia at the time. In her absence Governor McLean asked Lieutenant Governor and Mrs. J. Elmer Long to stand in their places.

Although Angus Wilton McLean was inaugurated governor in January 1925, Mrs. McLean and the couple's three children did not arrive in Raleigh until April of that year. During the months between the inauguration and his family's arrival, Governor McLean had arranged to have the Executive Mansion evaluated for extensive renovation. Inspections uncovered problems involving heating, plumbing, and cleanliness at the residence. When the few furnishings were found to be in disrepair, Harry Pier Giavina, a professional interior decorator of Wilmington, worked with Mrs. McLean on the interior repairs; those improvements took nearly two years to complete.

The McLeans were married on April 14, 1904, following a seven-year courtship. The intimate wedding was held in the Robeson County home of Mrs. McLean's maternal grandparents, Berry and Martha Faulk Godwin. After Margaret's parents, James McD. and Edna

Godwin French, divorced, her grandparents reared her. Her mother remarried and moved to Greensboro, leaving Margaret and her brother with their grandparents. Her lengthy courtship with Angus Wilton McLean began when he was beginning his law practice and she was attending the North Carolina State Normal and Industrial College (now the University of North Carolina at Greensboro). She went on to advanced studies at a music conservatory in Boston.

Margaret McLean guarded her privacy and that of her family, finding it hard to become close to people. She was very reserved and dignified in her manner, and her strict upbringing served her well as the wife of a prominent businessman and public servant. She was accustomed to formality and propriety in her relations with household staff and guests alike.

By 1908 the McLeans had built Duart House, their majestic neoclassic, columned mansion, on the site of the former Godwin family home. Within the walls of that elegant house they reared their three children. Angus Wilton II was born on January 13, 1913 (died October 21, 1996), Margaret French (Mrs. W. Scott Shepherd) in September 1915, and Hector (later married Lyl Warwick) on September 15, 1920. Because of the grand scale (ten thousand square feet) of their home, entertaining and hosting overnight guests were frequent occurrences. Mrs. McLean took great pride in gracious and creative events, from holiday and birthday parties to business and organizational meetings. She also enjoyed experimenting with foods and creating recipes. Although she did not cook, she could instruct others.

Mrs. McLean brought at least one servant, Rosetta Ross Martin, with her to the mansion, and Ms. Martin took care of young Hector. The first lady inspired servants to expand their abilities. A butler known as Uncle Dave began arranging flowers with a very creative flair. There was no housekeeper, so Margaret McLean executed the planning of events and purchasing of household supplies. A secretary, probably from the governor's office, was loaned to her to assist in addressing invitations.

McLean family portrait. From left—Governor McLean, holding Hector; Margaret French (seated on ground); Mrs. McLean, beside Angus Wilton II

The first lady supplemented the furnishings and table settings with the McLeans' own collection of china, silver, and crystal. She established a dining area on the second floor of the Executive Mansion so that the family could eat together upstairs. She also had the open east porch over the garage screened so that the family could sit there in comfort and privacy.

Margaret McLean never made public speeches but did make a few public appearances with her husband. She had formal teas for the calling public on Wednesday afternoons.

Ballroom transformed into an elaborate garden

Traditionally, entertaining at the mansion was done in categories—legislators in one group and ministers in another, and so on. Mrs. McLean decided to mix various types of people and found it more interesting for her guests. She had an innate sense of correctness and style that served her well. Her dramatic flair and taste were well known, and she thoroughly enjoyed being around some of the important guests such as President and Mrs. Calvin Coolidge and entertainer Will Rogers.

Three parties illustrate her skills. One was a statewide traditional New Year's Eve reception and open house for which she decorated the dining room table with a complex snow scene; three thousand guests attended. Another was a springtime event for the United Daughters of the Confederacy at which the ballroom was transformed into an elaborate garden complete with trees, scrubs, flowers, and fountain. In honoring invited Daughters of the American Revolution, Mrs. McLean decided to entertain them on George Washington's birthday and decorated the dining room table with a realistic depiction of Washington crossing the Delaware River. Following her large and elaborate parties, she allowed the children to have their own parties before the decorations were removed.

After leaving the governor's office, Mr. and Mrs. McLean and their children returned to Lumberton. Shortly, thereafter, they moved to Washington, D.C., where the former governor set up a law practice. The family traveled by train to Lumberton each weekend so that Mr. McLean could study the books of his other businesses. Partially because of that stressful schedule, his health deteriorated, and he died on June 21, 1935, of heart problems. Margaret McLean and the children moved back to their home in Lumberton.

Dining Room decorated with snow scene for New Year's Eve

Mrs. McLean, having lost contact with her mother in her youth, began visiting her in Greensboro and reestablished their relationship before her mother's death in 1939. Margaret McLean died on November 1, 1959, and was buried in Lumberton's Meadowbrook Cemetery. A contemporary newspaper article described her as having "a gentle and friendly simplicity which is the outward and visible sign of her genuine kindness."

Fay Lamar Webb Gardner

1929–1933

SEPTEMBER 7, 1885–JANUARY 16, 1969

Fay Lamar Webb, born September 7, 1885, into the prominent Webb family of Shelby, North Carolina, was the younger of two daughters born to Judge James Landrum Webb and Kansas Love Andrews Webb. The Webb family had long been politically active in the Shelby area, and "Miss Fay" certainly continued the tradition. She attended Shelby public schools and later Lucy Cobb School for Girls in Athens, Georgia, from which she graduated with honors in 1905. Afterward she spent two years traveling in Europe before marrying Oliver Maxwell Gardner on November 6, 1907.

Following her marriage to the busy lawyer, Fay Gardner became both helpmate for her politically active husband and businesswoman and civic leader in her own right. The Red Cross, the Garden Club of Shelby, the Cleveland County Historical Association, the Business and Professional Women's Club, the North Carolina Democratic Committee, and the National Women's Democratic Club were just a few of the organizations to which she belonged. She was also a member of the Daughters of the American Revolution, the United Daughters of the Confederacy, and the Colonial Dames of America. She and her husband worked to rejuvenate the flagging Boiling Springs Junior College. So successful were they in that effort that in 1942 the school was renamed Gardner-Webb College. Mr. and Mrs. Gardner also endowed several scholarships and spearheaded numerous fund-raising efforts on behalf of the college.

While in the Executive Mansion Fay Gardner gained the reputation for being a most gracious hostess. Indeed, she was as beloved a social leader in Raleigh as she had been in Shelby. Among those entertained at the Executive Mansion during her husband's term of office were

Governor and Mrs. Gardner (far right) with presidential candidate Al Smith and his wife in front of the Executive Mansion

Franklin and Eleanor Roosevelt, Charles Lindbergh, and Eddie Rickenbacker. In addition to her social activities, Mrs. Gardner was an active civic leader. One of her projects—subsequently developed further by succeeding first ladies and governors—was to create a rose garden at the state penitentiary. After hearing about a prisoner who enjoyed gardening, she asked to see him and learned that he liked roses. Accompanying him outside to a clear area, Mrs. Gardner supervised the digging of a garden and the planting of twenty rose plants. The twenty roses did so well that she ordered eighty more and soon diversified the garden with additional types of plants. The blossoms soon adorned the Executive Mansion rooms, and Mrs. Gardner noticed the change in the prisoner whose talents were directed into such useful and rewarding channels.

The Gardners were the parents of four children. Margaret Love Gardner was born in 1908 and later married Nathaniel E. Burgess and had two children. James Webb was born in 1910, subsequently married Iris Rollins, and had two children. Ralph Webb was born in 1912 and later married Josephine Bourne and secondly Carrie Horn Derby; he had one child. Oliver Maxwell Gardner Jr. was born in 1922 and later married Sara Hoyle Mull and had two children.

Mrs. Gardner at inauguration ceremony

After the Gardners left the governorship they went immediately to Washington, D.C., where the former governor opened a law practice. Just as she had become a favorite of society in Raleigh, Mrs. Gardner soon became a popular hostess in the nation's capital. Both were active socially and politically, and Fay Gardner remained so after the death of her husband on February 6, 1947, the morning they were to have departed for England following Max Gardner's appointment as ambassador to the Court of St. James.

Governor Dan K. Moore, Dr. William C. Friday, and Mrs. Gardner presenting the O. Max Gardner Award to Dr. Walton C. Gregory in 1967

After her husband's death, Mrs. Gardner continued to be active in civic and social events in Shelby and throughout the state. She traveled extensively with a widowed friend and maintained the family's relationship with Gardner-Webb College. Fay Gardner remained keenly interested in all levels of politics and traveled often between Shelby, Raleigh, and Washington. She was named Business and Professional Women's Woman of the Year for 1961. On that occasion she was quoted in the *Greensboro Record* (February 12, 1962): "'This is the summit honor of my life coming from these people whom I love—my hometown people.'"

Fay Gardner died January 16, 1969, in a Charlotte hospital after suffering a stroke six days earlier. She was buried in Sunset Cemetery in Shelby. An obituary published in the Raleigh *News and Observer* (January 17, 1969) reported that when Senator B. Everett Jordan heard of Mrs. Gardner's death, he declared: "very literally this marks the end of an era for North Carolina." Governor Bob Scott agreed, adding that "she was a grand lady all her life. . . . North Carolina has lost one of its finest citizens."

Matilda Bradford Haughton Ehringhaus
1933–1937

OCTOBER 23, 1890–JUNE 16, 1980

Outgoing and cheerful, Matilda "Tillie" Ehringhaus was a breath of fresh air in the depression-era administration of Governor J. C. B. Ehringhaus. With unflagging wit and good humor, she represented a pleasant diversion from the stress and strain of public life.

Matilda Bradford was born to Episcopal minister Thomas Benbury Haughton and Susan Elizabeth Lamb Haughton on October 23, 1890, in Williamston, Martin County. When Matilda was four, her father died, and the family moved to Washington, North Carolina. She later attended St. Mary's Junior College, from which she received a business certificate in 1908 and worked as a secretary until her marriage. On January 4, 1912, she married John Christoph Blucher Ehringhaus at St. Peter's Episcopal Church in Washington, North Carolina. Following their marriage they lived in Elizabeth City, where her husband practiced law.

Three children were born to J. C. B. and Tillie Ehringhaus. John Christoph Blucher Ehringhaus Jr. was the oldest, born March 8, 1913; he later married Margaret Irwin Peoples. He was followed by twins, Matilda and Haughton, who were born September 5, 1916. Daughter Matilda subsequently married James Telfair Cordon and had three children; son Haughton later married Johnny Walker and had two children.

Because of the financial strain of the Great Depression, the inauguration was very simple. The legislature appropriated only six hundred dollars for the event. The new governor and his wife welcomed the simplicity of the ceremony inasmuch as he had only recently been released from the hospital after having undergone treatment for a kidney infection and had to return to bed immediately afterward. While living at the Executive Mansion, Tillie Ehringhaus hosted many musical evenings during which her husband played the piano and the family and guests gathered around and sang. One of the first things Governor Ehringhaus did to help the depressed economy was to reduce his own salary. His wife immediately followed suit by lowering the wattage in the chandeliers and almost halving the electric bill at the mansion. In order to have enough silver to serve guests, Mrs. Ehringhaus, like other first ladies, brought her own to the Executive Mansion.

Mrs. Ehringhaus was never a particularly political person, though she enjoyed her years at the Executive Mansion. An article published in the Raleigh *News and Observer* on February 8, 1957, quoted her as remarking: "'It's an experience I'm glad I had, but I wouldn't want to be a governor's wife two terms.'" In a later article that appeared in the *Greensboro Record* (February 13, 1962), she noted that she had viewed with alarm her husband's decision to run for governor inasmuch as she did not enjoy the limelight. In spite of her reservations, the charming Mrs. Ehringhaus performed her duties with great style and made many lasting friends in the capital city. In its issue of August 26, 1933, *The State* magazine said: "[I]f they ever have a beauty contest among governors' wives, our Tilly will take the loving cup, or the medal, or whatever it is that they give as first prizes in contests of this nature."

While Mr. Ehringhaus was serving in the General Assembly in 1932, the family had lived at the Sir Walter Hotel in Raleigh. At the conclusion of his term of office as governor in January 1937, he and his family moved to a house on Fairview Road in Raleigh. In 1946 they returned to the Sir Walter Hotel. There the former governor died in 1949. Mrs. Ehringhaus remained at the hotel for several years. Along with a friend, she edited the *North Carolina Almanac* and compiled the *State Industrial Guide*. In 1954 she moved to a small farm outside Edenton, where some of her family resided. She remodeled her house, and for a time two of her grandchildren lived with her and attended school in Edenton. She remained on her farm for twenty years before moving back to Raleigh, where she lived until her death.

Dinner party in Executive Mansion Dining Room. At left end of table—Governor and Mrs. Ehringhaus, Governor Hoey, trusty Clarence McMillan (standing); at right end—Mrs. Hoey, Mrs. Gardner, Governor Cherry, butler David Haywood (standing)

Matilda Ehringhaus died in Raleigh on June 16, 1980, at the age of eighty-nine. She was buried beside her husband in the Christ Episcopal Church Cemetery in Elizabeth City.

Margaret Elizabeth Gardner Hoey

1937–1941

JANUARY 21, 1875–FEBRUARY 13, 1942

The only first lady of North Carolina to be the wife of one governor (Clyde R. Hoey) and the sister of another (O. Max Gardner) was "Bess" Hoey. Margaret Elizabeth Gardner was born January 21, 1875, in Shelby to Dr. Oliver Perry Gardner and Margaret Young Gardner. Dr. Gardner was a widely respected country physician and prominent civic leader. At the time of her mother's death, Bess Gardner, then age sixteen, was a student at Shelby Female College; she soon became a surrogate mother to her younger brothers, and the care of children became a hallmark of her life.

On March 22, 1900, Bess married Clyde Roark Hoey, and they eventually became the parents of three children. Clyde R. Hoey Jr. was born January 19, 1901, and later married Bernice Hamrick and had one son; after Bernice died, he married Ruth Moore. Charles Aycock Hoey was born September 17, 1902, and subsequently married Mary Gidney and had two daughters and a son. Isabel Young Hoey was born January 26, 1907, and, a few months after her mother's death, married Daniel M. Paul; the Pauls had two sons.

Although Bess Hoey taught for a time before her marriage, she preferred the role of wife and mother and viewed it as her greatest calling. After her husband was elected governor, she brought her nurturing, generous love of people to the Executive Mansion. Even before their move to Raleigh, Mrs. Hoey had made a name for herself as a speaker and was much in demand among various civic organizations. Her sphere of influence broadened to the entire state after her husband became governor. While Governor Hoey had a reputation as an excellent orator, his wife obviously had much the same gift. She spoke often on the subjects of highway beautification, women's roles, and the welfare of children. All her life Bess Hoey enjoyed amateur dramatics. As the *Raleigh Times* (January 7, 1937) remarked: "North Carolina's new first lady, Mrs. Clyde Roark Hoey[,] graciously gay, witty and sympathetic, brings with her to the Executive Mansion a multiplicity of interests and experiences. Her popularity in the western part of the state—her home—is due to her exceptional love for people, her hospitality and her outstanding personality."

Mrs. Hoey certainly had the opportunity to exercise her skills as an accomplished hostess at the many teas, receptions, and dinners over which she presided while in Raleigh. The Hoeys' daughter Isabel, who lived with them, often shared hostess duties with her mother. Bess often employed her considerable talents as a cook. An article in the *Charlotte Observer* (February 14, 1942) said of Bess Hoey: "It was a plain, old-fashioned, homey household in which the humblest were heartily welcomed and quickly came to feel at ease in its congenial and affable fellowships. It was Mrs. Hoey who carried [to], and made to preside in the Mansion, the spirit of the common people, the social democracy of the commonwealth."

Mrs. Hoey and daughter Isabel attending a picnic at the Coastal Plains Test Farm

Bess Hoey, always active in civic, social, and religious organizations, belonged to the United Daughters of the Confederacy and the Daughters of the American Revolution, as well as the Twentieth Century Book Club and Community Players. She served also as president of the Woman's Club in Shelby. For many years she taught Sunday school and was so popular as a teacher that the class often had more than sixty members. One of Mrs. Hoey's most lasting interests was in gardening, and her garden in Shelby was renowned for its beauty. She brought that interest with her to the Executive Mansion, watching over the mansion gardens and creating a greenhouse for exotic flowers at the state penitentiary. The *Greensboro Daily News* (December 13, 1936) quoted her as saying: "'My family was certainly named right, we were all born gardeners. My father was a doctor but he only practiced medicine for a living; he farmed for fun.'"

Governor and Mrs. Hoey and daughter Isabel with others in receiving line at the Executive Mansion

Mrs. Hoey working at her desk in the Executive Mansion

Margaret Elizabeth Gardner Hoey died suddenly of a heart attack on February 13, 1942, about thirteen months after her husband's term of office had ended and the couple had returned to Shelby. Mrs. Hoey was buried at Sunset Cemetery in Shelby. After her death, her devastated husband always wore a red rose or carnation in his lapel to honor her. Her husband's will established the Bess Gardner Hoey Memorial Fund, a trust administered for charitable, educational, and religious purposes. Bess Hoey did not live to see her husband, unique in his everyday attire of English walking coat, striped trousers, high starched collar, and flower in his lapel, become a United States senator in 1945.

Alice Harper Willson Broughton

1941–1945

JULY 13, 1889 – AUGUST 15, 1980

While Alice Willson Broughton was not the first North Carolina first lady from Wake County, the Broughtons were the first and only governor and first lady to live in the Executive Mansion who were both Wake County natives. Her husband, Joseph Melville Broughton, also has the distinction of being the only governor in the state's history to be a native of Raleigh.

Alice Harper Willson was born July 13, 1889, the daughter of William W. and Alice Partin Willson. Alice Willson Broughton's roots ran deep in Raleigh, Wake County, and state history. Her father was city clerk of Raleigh and secretary of the Grand Lodge of Masons of North Carolina. Her mother was a public schoolteacher. A great uncle, Donald Bain, was state treasurer for many years.

Alice Broughton, who was one of four children, often remembered the joys of growing up in Raleigh. She recalled fondly the occasions when she was awakened by her father who had brought oysters home from the Masonic lodge to share with her. She also remembered meeting her father on a corner near their home where he got off the streetcar after a day's work. Even as a child Alice Willson would be up and out of bed early. For much of her childhood, she had private music lessons each morning at 7:30. Her teacher was Professor Levin, who had been a well-known German musician. He believed that music, like much else, could be best mastered early in the day while the mind was fresh. Alice carried that idea with her throughout her life. As a young woman, she continued her education in her hometown, attending Peace College.

Mrs. Eleanor Roosevelt, Governor and Mrs. Broughton, President Roosevelt during a visit to Raleigh

Alice Willson knew her future husband, Melville Broughton, all through school, but their romance did not begin until a hayride with a group of young people from Tabernacle Baptist Sunday School when Broughton was a student at Wake Forest College. On December 14, 1916, they were married. At that time, he was a young lawyer, and she worked in the circulation department of a Raleigh newspaper, a position she held for eight years.

Alice Willson and her family were strong Methodists. After she married Mr. Broughton, however, she followed him to Tabernacle Baptist Church. There they worked together in many areas of the church, including the twenty-six years during which Mr. Broughton was Sunday School superintendent.

The Broughtons always discussed things with each other before making major decisions. When Mr. Broughton considered running for governor he asked for her opinion. She responded, "I think you are fine enough to be governor, and if you think it is the thing to do, I feel that no greater honor can come to a man than being governor of his own state." During the campaign, as she drove him around the state, they engaged in intellectual conversations. At their appointed stops, while he spoke to the crowds about the issues, she crocheted. By the end of the campaign, she had crocheted an entire bedspread.

The Broughton family moved into the Executive Mansion in January 1941 with four children: Alice Willson (August 30, 1919–July 27, 1977); Joseph Melville Jr. (March 24, 1922–

April 17, 1997), who married Mary Ann Cooper; Robert Bain (born November 28, 1924), who married Celeste Gold and subsequently, Sumner Parham); and Woodson Harris (December 20, 1927–April 16, 1979). Woodson, the youngest, was thirteen and the most resistant to moving from his Raleigh home to the mansion. Woodson asked his mother if they could rent the governor's mansion to someone else and remain in their own home. He adapted rather well, however, as one of Mrs. Broughton's first acts was to turn a third-floor room into a clubroom for his Boy Scout troop.

Christening the ship named for Donald Bain, Mrs. Broughton's great uncle

The Broughtons' term in the mansion, like that of the Bicketts a quarter century earlier, was dominated by a world war. Alice Broughton assisted in the war effort in many ways. She even carefully apportioned the food served at the mansion, including the traditional breakfasts served to General Assembly members. When word got out that meals at the governor's mansion were affected by wartime rationing, citizens from across the state sent the food stamps necessary to purchase many food items. Alice Broughton welcomed servicemen into the mansion for weekend visits, just as Mrs. Bickett had done during World War I. Mrs. Broughton promoted the national rubber drive by stripping fifty-eight pounds of rubber tread from the service staircase in the mansion and personally taking it to a collection center. She frequently christened Liberty ships that had been built at Wilmington. She also promoted victory gardens by tending one herself on the mansion grounds. The Broughtons boosted the morale of servicemen by inviting them to be overnight guests at the Executive Mansion.

Mrs. Broughton promoting North Carolina peaches

Some important changes were made at the mansion during the Broughtons' stay. In 1941 an elevator was installed in an area within the service staircase. A beautiful state silver service, designed and engraved by silversmiths Fred Starke of Connecticut and Clarence Bowman of Raleigh, was created. It included the state seal, pine boughs, dogwood, and other symbols of North Carolina. Alice Broughton, in looking back on her time in the mansion, always considered the acquisition of the silver service to be one of her most lasting accomplishments.

Beginning in 1941 and especially the following year, Mrs. Broughton and her husband were extensively involved with legislation to establish and promote both a state-sponsored symphony orchestra (now known as the North Carolina Symphony) and a state art gallery (now known as the North Carolina Museum of Art). Mrs. Broughton's patronage of those institutions continued throughout her tenure as first lady and for many years thereafter. She was appointed to the Tryon Palace Commission in 1950 and maintained a deep commitment to that body throughout her life.

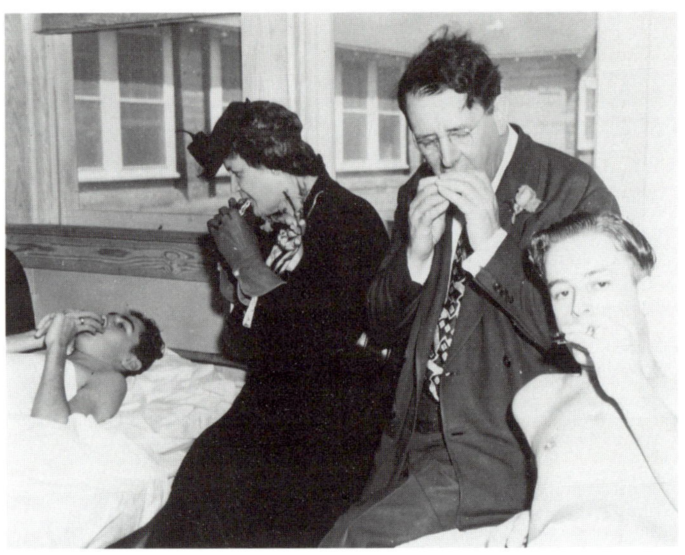

Governor and Mrs. Broughton playing harmonica with men in hospital

After completing his term as governor, Melville Broughton ran successfully for the U.S. Senate in 1948 against his good friend William B. Umstead. The stress of the campaign seemed to tax his strength, however. On March 6, 1949, only months after taking office, he died. Alice Broughton moved back to her home in Raleigh's Hayes Barton neighborhood and lived there until her death on August 15, 1980, at the age of ninety-one. Alice Harper Willson Broughton was buried in Raleigh's Montlawn Memorial Park.

During her long and productive life, Alice Willson Broughton's interests and activities were varied. She was a member of the Raleigh Garden Club, the Daughters of the American Revolution, the Needlework Guild, the Woman's Club of Raleigh, and the Raleigh Little Theatre. She also belonged to the Roanoke Island Historical Association, the North Carolina Antiquities Society, and the North Carolina Art Society. While her children were growing up, she was active in the Parent-Teacher Association. Mrs. Broughton also served on the North Carolina Democratic Executive Committee, the North Carolina Prison Advisory Council, and the Wake Forest University Board of Trustees. Upon her death, a close personal friend, Dan Sapp, rector of Christ Episcopal Church, said, "Mrs. Broughton's primary interest was in people."

Mildred Stafford Cherry

1945–1949

AUGUST 8, 1894–APRIL 10, 1971

Gregarious and gracious, Mildred Cherry met the challenges of being a governor's wife with her customary good nature. She found the first lady's duties challenging, but she easily adapted her schedule to that of her busy husband and to the accelerated pace of social and political activities in Raleigh. The *Gastonia Gazette* of April 12, 1971, quoted Mrs. Cherry as saying that she had "enjoyed most the many interesting people whom she and the Governor entertained there. Among these personalities were Eleanor Roosevelt, General Dwight Eisenhower, President and Mrs. Harry Truman and their daughter, Margaret, and Josephus Daniels, ambassador to Mexico."

During the Cherry administration the mansion staff underwent changes. Laura M. Reilley, the official housekeeper, hostess, and staff supervisor of the Executive Mansion, helped Mrs. Cherry schedule events and manage the large household. David Haywood, affectionately known as Uncle Dave, longtime butler at the mansion, died on November 21, 1947. He had served fourteen governors and their families for fifty-four years.

Mildred Stafford was born August 8, 1894, in Statesville but moved to Greensboro when only a year old. She was one of Emory J. and Lula Roberta Lowry Stafford's seven children. Her father served two terms (1909 and 1917) as mayor of Greensboro. She attended public schools in that city and graduated from Greensboro High School, where she greatly enjoyed playing basketball. Later she attended Greensboro College for two years and Randolph-Macon Women's College in Lynchburg, Virginia. Mildred Stafford taught second grade in the Greensboro City Schools until she met and married Robert Gregg Cherry, lawyer and then

Governor and Mrs. Cherry congratulating North Carolina Symphony conductor Dr. Benjamin Swalin following a performance

mayor of Gastonia. They met in Gastonia while she was attending a summer session of the Institute for Teachers. They were married in Greensboro on June 28, 1921. The Cherrys had no children.

After her marriage Mildred Cherry was active in the civic and social affairs of Gastonia. She was a member of the Daughters of the American Revolution, the Red Cross, and other organizations. She had a keen interest in gardening and reading. One of her hobbies was collecting china demitasse coffee cups and dessert plates, as well as other antique china. Her collection was vast.

Mrs. Cherry shared a strong interest in North Carolina with her husband and supported his service to the state—he was a member of the state legislature for several years. During World War II she led many activities in support of the war effort. She encouraged the sale of war bonds and helped in the appeal that gained the state its quota of 105 women for training as hospital technicians in the Women's Army Corps. Although peace was declared during the Cherrys' first year in the Executive Mansion, wartime shortages still prevailed. Mrs. Cherry's frugality kept entertaining costs within the $2,500 annual budget. Mildred Cherry preferred the simpler events for local groups and legislators to the lavish, expensive affairs necessary for national and international dignitaries.

While living in the Executive Mansion, Mrs. Cherry added her touch to the building's decor. She redecorated the Rose Room, the official guest room, as well as another guest room. She also chose new rugs and carpets for the second floor, but because of shortages of materials, she was unable to do the same for the first floor.

On June 14, 1944, the *Gastonia Gazette* said of her: "Governors may, and often do, fight their way to the high seat by means of natural endowments and hard apprenticeship in Governmental affairs, but First Ladies are born, not made. Such a lady was Mildred Cherry."

After their tenure in the Executive Mansion, the Cherrys returned to their many friends and activities in Gastonia. Upon her husband's death in 1957, Mrs. Cherry bought a new house and indulged two of her favorite hobbies—interior design and reading. In later years, Mrs. Cherry's health limited her role in the various organizations that had meant so much to her.

After suffering for some time with heart trouble, Mildred Cherry died in Gastonia on April 10, 1971, at age seventy-six. She was buried beside her husband in Gaston Memorial Park in Gastonia.

Mary Elizabeth White Scott

1949–1953

APRIL 30, 1897–APRIL 23, 1972

Having remained steadfast to the family farm at Haw River while her husband was commissioner of agriculture, Mary Elizabeth White Scott looked forward to the role of first lady in 1949. For eleven years, William Kerr Scott had served the citizens as commissioner before running for governor. During this time, "Miss Mary," as he affectionately called his wife, had been keeping the books and managing the dairy farm of thirteen hundred acres, as well as raising their three children: Osborne White, born September 27, 1920; Mary Kerr Scott, October 10, 1921, who later married Alfred Johnson Lowdermilk Jr.; and Robert Walter, June 13, 1929, who later married Jessie Rae Osborne.

One of seven children, Mary Elizabeth White was born on April 30, 1897, to the farming family of James Richard and Elizabeth Ann Sellers White. Living only a short distance from the Scott farm, she and her future husband walked to school and attended church and community activities together. After Mr. Scott spent two years in the army during World War I, he and Mary were married on July 2, 1919. They established their farm on 225 acres given to them by his father and lived there in an expanded three-room log house that they moved from her family's farm.

Mary Elizabeth White taught for a year to earn money to attend State Normal and Industrial College in Greensboro (now the University of North Carolina at Greensboro), where she took teacher training courses. She then taught at Woodlawn School in Alamance County, Anderson School in Caswell County, and at Taylorsville in Alexander County.

When time permitted, she enjoyed her hobbies of knitting, crocheting, and reading (from comics to Plato), but there was always time and the need for her favorites—gardening and cooking. Friends, extra family members, and business associates were often guests at mealtime.

Mrs. Scott's experiences during her years of teaching, church activities, work with home demonstration clubs, and as a charter member of the first North Carolina 4-H club readied her for a lifetime of leadership. She worked with others in her community to bring about rural electrification, good health practices and medical care, and rural telephone service. Without those basic improvements, as well as roads on which to transport goods to market, farms and rural communities would not grow and prosper.

The Winston-Salem *Journal* of April 26, 1972, pointed out that Mrs. Scott's "spirit and energy made her exceptional at a time when the world of politics considered most women ornamental, more for display than consultation. But she took pains to keep her influence a private matter and to remain part of the background as her husband's career reached out. . . ." Mr. Scott's first political race was for state commissioner of agriculture. He came home as often as he could but left the management of the farm—keeping financial records, registering purebred cattle, and repairing equipment—to his wife. She still made time, however, to attend national and regional meetings with him. When her husband decided to run for governor, Mrs. Scott was there when he needed her, working tirelessly behind the scenes. All of those experiences helped prepare her for the role of first lady. Her ability to get things done, organize, manage financial matters, and make decisions on her own would stand her in good stead in Raleigh.

While first lady, "Miss Mary" made everyone feel at home and relaxed in the Executive Mansion. Her personal graciousness and charm were ever present. Having entertained a vast variety of guests in their Hawfields home, Mrs. Scott was at ease with preparing food and managing a household. In addition, she had the ready assistance of Laura M. Reilley, manager and hostess, as well as seven prisoners assigned to the official residence. During Governor Scott's four years in office, more than 225,000 people visited the mansion.

Mrs. Scott entertaining a women's group in the Executive Mansion Dining Room

Mrs. Scott unexpectedly faced having to renovate and refurbish the Executive Mansion. The building had not been well maintained during the previous twenty-five years because of the world wars and the depression. After a review by the legislature and an outstanding committee of architects from State College's School of Design, fifty thousand dollars was appropriated for improvements. Updating the kitchen, repairing the leaking roof, and replacing exterior woodwork were the major renovations. The refurbishing of draperies, carpets, and furniture was undertaken with the consultation of interior decorator Anna Riddick.

Two years after leaving the Executive Mansion, Mrs. Scott made a home for herself and the newly elected senator in a suite at the Carroll Arms Hotel in Washington, D.C. Viewing and listening from the Senate galleries, Mrs. Scott learned about the great needs of the country and how the national government worked. She became active in the Senate ladies group that prepared bandages for the Red Cross and met to discuss issues of interest. That group was a ready source of social engagements and for making new friends and reestablishing old ones. Senator and Mrs. Scott always enjoyed visits from their constituents and even invited the Hawfields Presbyterian Church elders and deacons to meet in the Capitol dining room. Their tenure in Washington, D.C., was cut short when Senator Scott died in 1958.

Mrs. Scott arranging roses in the mansion

Mrs. Scott returned to Melville Farms in Alamance County to enjoy her grandchildren and her beloved community. She was also active with appointments to the State Board of Health and the North Carolina Hospitals Board of Control. She received many honors, including being named "Woman of the Year" by the *Progressive Farmer* in 1949 and the state Grange in 1951, an award of merit from the American Red Cross in 1952, and the Distinguished Service Award of the National Arthritis and Rheumatism Foundation in 1966. North Carolina State University recognized her in 1970 for her lifetime of contributions to the people of North Carolina. At Western Carolina University a dormitory was dedicated and named in her honor.

When Mrs. Scott, almost seventy-five years old, died of pneumonia on April 23, 1972, her son, then governor Robert Walter Scott, received friends at the Executive Mansion. The service and burial were at her beloved Hawfields Presbyterian Church and Cemetery. "Mary, the Queen of Scott's Land" was so admired that Secretary of State Thad Eure had the state flag flown at half-mast in her honor. A Raleigh *News and Observer* editorial of April 25, 1972, declared: "She was a quiet, gracious and strong woman who believed public service an obligation and thought principled conduct an unremarkable expectation." A North Carolina State University resolution, quoted in the same issue, praised her further: "In her many careers as teacher, mother, advisor to governors, and leader among her people, Mary Scott stood in the fullest sense for the great American dream of making the most of oneself to the betterment of others." Even in her last will and testament she continued to think of her cherished community, leaving sixty-two acres to Hawfields Presbyterian Church "to be used for the purpose of providing a rest home for the aged and needy of the Hawfields Church community." Such was the spirit of Mary Elizabeth White Scott.

Merle Holland Davis Umstead

1953–1954

JULY 11, 1901–APRIL 14, 1988

Merle Holland Davis Umstead was well prepared for the job of first lady. Her husband, William Bradley Umstead, had served three terms in Congress during the Franklin D. Roosevelt administration, as chairman of the State Democratic Executive Committee, and as a United States senator; as a result, Mrs. Umstead brought years of experience in political life to the Executive Mansion.

Merle Davis was born July 11, 1901, in Bostic in Rutherford County. Her parents, Charles Daniel and Daisy Washburn Davis, ran a store in the Sunshine community. After graduating in 1919 from the Normal and Collegiate Institute, an Asheville boarding school, she became a high school teacher and the principal at the Sunshine School in her native Rutherford County. From 1921 to 1922 she attended Trinity College (known as Duke University after 1924). After a year, she left school for employment in Raleigh with the Internal Revenue Service. She returned to Trinity College in 1923, however, and graduated with a degree in English in 1926.

While at Duke she took a job caring for the children of a prominent Durham family and became acquainted with one of her employers' relatives, a young Durham attorney named William B. Umstead. In 1926 she returned to Sunshine School as principal and then taught at Rutherfordton's Central High School. She continued to teach until she married William B. Umstead on September 5, 1929, at Durham's Trinity Methodist Church. Following the marriage, Merle Umstead engaged in numerous activities in Durham, including serving as president of the Durham American Legion Auxiliary and teaching Sunday School at Trinity. Just three years after their marriage, her husband ran for his first term in Congress.

While the Umsteads were in Washington, they resided at the Willard Hotel, a customary residence at the time for members of Congress and their spouses. A regular at congressional dinners and functions for congressional wives, Merle Umstead was active in Washington's social life. One of her favorite activities was giving guided tours of the city to friends and constituents from North Carolina.

William B. Umstead left the House after three terms in 1938 and then practiced law in Durham. In 1946 he was appointed to the U.S. Senate upon the death of Senator Josiah W. Bailey. During Umstead's term in the Senate, Mrs. Umstead maintained their residence in Durham, raising their young daughter, also named Merle, who was born in 1942. Mrs. Umstead and her daughter traveled to Washington frequently by train, however.

Senator Umstead was elected governor in 1952 and inaugurated on January 7, 1953. Just two days into his term, he suffered a heart attack. As a result, the first lady played an even more important role than usual in his administration, including being largely responsible for managing the governor's schedule. Governor Umstead held most of his appointments in the mansion, often around a table in his bedroom. Since his schedule was limited by his heart condition, Mrs. Umstead determined which invitations to accept and which to decline, and which events were important enough to work into the governor's limited schedule. Despite the unusual circumstances, Merle Davis Umstead managed the mansion beautifully, without problems or complaints, even though she did not have an office staff, social secretary, or appointments manager. Laura M. Reilley, housekeeper, and Mrs. Umstead's mother, Daisy Washburn Davis, were there to assist, however.

Grand march at inaugural ball for Governor Umstead. From left— Governor and Mrs. Umstead, Merle B. Umstead, Betsy Burnette, Lieutenant Governor Hodges, Mrs. Hodges, Nancy Hodges Finlay, and Luther Hodges Jr.

Mrs. Umstead (on right) with Mrs. D. S. Coltrane and Mrs. Karl Bishopric preparing for war bond drive

Merle D. Umstead treasured life in the mansion. She loved flower arranging and took delight in the fresh flowers that were frequently sent from the prison farm. She enjoyed giving tours of the mansion to school groups—seating the children on the grand staircase and telling them of the building's history and treasures. An early appreciation of antiques and heirlooms inspired her to collect Davis and Umstead family furniture and treasures—not so much for their monetary value as for their history. Mrs. Umstead was also interested in cooking. She always used the freshest ingredients available and took great pride in the preparation of dishes. She took cooking lessons and saved many menus and recipes from important events.

The Umsteads had planned to build a house in Durham when the governor left office. The governor's death on November 7, 1954, before the completion of his term, changed all of that. The first lady and their eleven-year-old daughter had to vacate the mansion almost immediately and were without a home. Mrs. Umstead never built the house she and her husband had planned but returned to Durham and eventually purchased a home designed by Durham architect George Watts Carr.

In the years following her husband's death, Merle Davis Umstead remained active in the public life of North Carolina. She was a longtime supporter of the Roanoke Island Historical Association and served as the Durham County leader of that organization for many years. From 1955 to 1961 she was a member of the East Carolina University Board of Trustees. Mrs. Umstead, who saved many of her husband's documents and maintained scrapbooks of their political careers, took an active role in the publication of the *Public Addresses, Letters, and Papers of William Bradley Umstead, Governor of North Carolina, 1953–1954*. She provided a home for many students attending Duke University and Durham Technical College. In addition, she actively managed family timberland in Rutherford County.

Mrs. Umstead lived in her home in Durham until her death on April 14, 1988. She was buried beside her husband at Mt. Tabor United Methodist Church in northern Durham County, where Governor Umstead had grown up.

Merle Davis Umstead is survived by her only child, daughter Merle B. Umstead Richey, a Durham attorney and the wife of Russell E. Richey, and two grandchildren, William, born in 1970, and Elizabeth, born in 1977.

Martha Elizabeth Blakeney Hodges
1954–1961

SEPTEMBER 12, 1897–JUNE 27, 1969

Martha Blakeney was born September 12, 1897, and grew up in Monroe in Union County. Her parents, Rochel Edward and Margaret Houston Blakeney, died when she was young, and Martha and her five sisters went to live with their maternal grandmother, Susan Covington Houston. Mrs. Houston also lived in Monroe; consequently, the girls could remain in the familiar surroundings of their hometown. Their grandmother was well educated, and she tutored Martha and her sisters. Unfortunately, Mrs. Houston died in 1913, and once more the Blakeney children had to move. This time they went to live with Mr. and Mrs. Richard Brewer, an aunt and uncle who resided in Wake Forest. From 1914 to 1918 Martha Blakeney attended State Normal and Industrial College in Greensboro (now the University of North Carolina at Greensboro). After graduation, she taught for three years at Leaksville-Spray High School and during the last year served as principal as well. She also taught at a Greensboro high school for a year. While at Leaksville-Spray High School, she met Luther Hartwell Hodges, an official at Marshall Field Mills. They were married June 24, 1922. She continued to teach after their marriage and did graduate work at Columbia University and at the University of Chicago.

Luther and Martha Hodges had three children. Betsy Blakeney was born June 11, 1925. She married Donald M. Bernard Jr., and they had three children. Nancy Houston, born September 28, 1926, became the wife of John Campbell Finlay and the mother of four children. Luther Hodges Jr., born November 19, 1936, married Dorothy Duncan, and they had two children. He subsequently married Cheray Zauderer.

Luther Hodges Sr. left Marshall Field Mills in 1950 and became chief of the industry division of the Economic Cooperation Administration in West Germany, where he and his wife lived. Mrs. Hodges later traveled even more extensively, visiting various parts of the world. Hodges became lieutenant governor in 1952 and governor in 1954 when Governor William B. Umstead died in office. Hodges would later win a full term of his own.

While her husband was governor, Martha Hodges entertained often. As first lady she hosted teas, dinners, and musicals for many civic groups visiting the Executive Mansion. A steady stream of dignitaries was likewise entertained at the mansion. A tradition existed by which groups meeting in Raleigh expected to be invited to the mansion. Mrs. Hodges thought some order had to be brought to that custom, and a policy for tour hours and social gatherings was developed. Mrs. Hodges also had a part-time secretary to help with scheduling and correspondence.

Mrs. Hodges's other duties as first lady included traveling with the governor, attending ribbon-cutting ceremonies, arranging the many flowers used in the large residence, and managing the mansion household and gardens. She particularly enjoyed the gardens, and flower arranging was one of her favorite hobbies. Laura M. Reilley helped to manage the mansion and oversaw hostessing duties; she retired to her Charlotte home when the Hodges administration ended.

Mrs. Hodges with her grandchildren. She is holding Donald Bernard III; on her left is Martha Bernard; top to bottom on her right—Vary Finlay, Carol Bernard, Vivian Finlay

Before her husband became governor, Martha Hodges enjoyed playing bridge, reading, and painting, and she continued to do so when time permitted after moving into the mansion. A lifelong learner, she took pleasure in attending weekly art history lectures at the North Carolina Museum of Art.

While she had hoped that her husband would retire when his term ended, Mrs. Hodges supported his decision to accept President John F. Kennedy's appointment as secretary of commerce. Though their lives in Washington, D.C., were similar in many ways to what they had been in the Executive Mansion, Mrs. Hodges's domestic life was somewhat simpler with only a two-bedroom apartment to maintain. While living in Washington she was president of the International Neighbors Club, an organization of the wives of ambassadors, congressmen, senators, and government officials, which afforded her a cosmopolitan circle of friends. Governor Hodges served in the cabinets of John F. Kennedy and Lyndon B. Johnson, and he and Mrs. Hodges were personal friends with both men and their wives.

In 1965 Luther and Martha Hodges moved to Chapel Hill, where they had previously bought a house. That house was important to Mrs. Hodges. With her children married with children of their own and scattered around the world, she wanted a base where they could be together as a family. The house became that for them, but it was also the scene of a tragedy. On June 26, 1969, the house caught fire. The former governor was injured in jumping from a second-floor window. Martha Hodges was later found unconscious in a first-floor bedroom. The following day she died of smoke inhalation and asphyxiation complicated by respiratory and cardiac problems. Seventy-one years old at the time of her death, Mrs. Hodges was buried in Eden's Overlook Cemetery in Rockingham County.

Governor and Mrs. Hodges at the North Carolina Museum of Art opening

Governor and Mrs. Hodges board airplane for trade mission

Margaret Rose Knight Sanford

1961–1965

JUNE 6, 1918

Margaret Rose Knight was born on June 6, 1918, in Hopkinsville in Christian County, Kentucky. Her parents, John Richard and Elizabeth Ford Knight, died when she and her brother John were young, and she was reared by an aunt, Hettie Dickson. Margaret Rose Knight attended Christian College in Columbia, Missouri, and then transferred to the University of North Carolina at Chapel Hill, from which she graduated in 1941. Although she came to Chapel Hill because of the drama department, she changed majors and graduated with a degree in English. It was there that she met her husband, James Terry Sanford. They were married July 4, 1942, at Hettie Dickson's home in Hopkinsville, just before he enlisted in the army as a paratrooper. She had taught in the Chatham County public schools the year before the marriage. During World War II, while her husband was overseas, Mrs. Sanford returned to Kentucky, where she continued to teach.

Margaret Rose Sanford brought with her to the Executive Mansion a naturalness and warmth that became a hallmark of her tenure. A tribute to Mrs. Sanford by a political reporter in the *Raleigh Times* of December 4, 1964, stated: "'She always seemed to be bubbling over with good cheer. She has a spontaneous wit.'"

Mrs. Sanford was the mother of two preteen children, Betsee, eleven, and James Terry Jr., eight, when the Sanfords came to Raleigh from Fayetteville, and she was determined to rear them as naturally as she could. The Sanfords enrolled their children in public schools and tried to maintain as normal a routine for them as possible. Governor Sanford did not take the children to school on their first day because he knew that photographers and reporters would accompany him. Such an entourage would have disrupted the school day. Mrs. Sanford regretted that official duties kept her from spending as much time with the children as she would have liked. Overall, however, she believed that the children's experiences in Raleigh were positive. The Sanfords were family oriented, and they frequently invited Mrs. Sanford's niece, who was attending St. Mary's Junior College in Raleigh, to spend weekends at the Executive Mansion.

Governor and Mrs. Sanford with Metropolitan Opera soprano Eleanor Steber and her husband, Gordon Andrews, at the 1963 North Carolina Symphony Ball at the Executive Mansion

Music, books, and flowers were an important part of life in the Executive Mansion during the Sanford administration. Just before moving to Raleigh, Mrs. Sanford began taking violin lessons, something she had long wanted to do. From childhood she had played the piano, a skill she encouraged in her daughter. Mrs. Sanford also played the organ. The Sanfords held the first North Carolina Symphony Ball in 1961. Both the Sanfords were avid readers and began a library of North Carolina books for the mansion. Mrs. Sanford also started the rose garden in the northwest corner of the mansion grounds, at the intersection of Blount and Lane Streets, where it continues today.

Governor and Mrs. Sanford celebrating the tercentenary of the granting of North Carolina Charter from King Charles II to the Lords Proprietors (1663)

While the Sanfords resided in the Executive Mansion, the state was given a house near Asheville to be the governor's Western Residence. The house was to serve as a retreat for the first family, as well as a place where state officials could stay when in the area. As first lady, Mrs. Sanford enjoyed traveling with her husband, particularly to the various governors' conferences held around the United States.

From Raleigh the family returned to Fayetteville with their two teenagers, and then to Durham when Terry Sanford became president of Duke University. Always supportive of her

Governor and Mrs. Sanford with singer Eddie Arnold and schoolchildren in the Executive Mansion Ballroom

husband's ambitions, Margaret Rose Sanford handled their new position just as she had their move to the Executive Mansion. Although Governor Sanford initially did not intend to remain as Duke's president for so long, he continued in the post for sixteen years. During that time Mrs. Sanford served on the board of the Methodist Home for Children in Raleigh and the board of trustees at East Carolina University. She was a member of the Defense Advisory Committee for Women in Service, the Education Commission of the States, the North Carolina Symphony Board, the Stagville Restoration Board, and the board of the North Carolina School of the Arts. Governor James B. Hunt Jr. appointed her to the delegation of Duke faculty and administration to visit the People's Republic of China in 1975.

Margaret Rose Sanford accompanied her husband to Washington, D.C., in 1987 when he began his term in the U.S. Senate. The political and social schedules were hectic, but the Sanfords tried to spend their weekends at home in Durham.

When Terry Sanford retired from Duke in 1986, he and Mrs. Sanford moved into a newly built home near Duke's west campus. They had designed the house themselves, and their son, Terry Jr.'s, construction company had built it. Mrs. Sanford continues to live in the house since the death of her husband on April 18, 1998. In April 1999 she and her children and grandchildren attended a White House ceremony at which President Bill Clinton signed a bill naming the Raleigh Federal Building after Terry Sanford. The family also attended the dedication ceremony in Raleigh in August of that year. Margaret Rose Sanford has a very special talent for making friends. People of all ages who have known her and her late husband through the years and many who were protégés of the governor gather around her and maintain close contact with her.

Jeanelle Coulter Moore

1965–1969

JULY 13, 1911–OCTOBER 20, 1999

All of North Carolina's first ladies who have lived in the Executive Mansion have in some way left their personal mark, whether it was a grand piece of furniture, silver, or their special hospitality. None has left a more lasting imprint that Jeanelle Coulter Moore, wife of Governor Daniel Killian Moore. The mansion's present beauty, grace, charm, and perhaps its continued existence as the governor's official residence, are a credit to Mrs. Moore.

Jeanelle Coulter was not a native of her beloved North Carolina; she was born in Pikeville, Tennessee, on July 13, 1911, the daughter of Coy Hixson and Margaret Colvard Coulter. She attended the University of Tennessee briefly before transferring to Western Carolina Teachers College in Cullowhee (now Western Carolina University), where she received her degree in education. In 1931, while visiting relatives in western North Carolina and taking a summer course at Western Carolina, she attended a local church. On that particular Sunday morning, she met the Sunday School superintendent, whom she described as the most handsome man she had ever seen. On May 4, 1933, Jeanelle Coulter and Dan Moore were married. Jeanelle Moore briefly taught second grade in Sylva in western North Carolina until the birth of Edith Coulter Moore, the first of their two children. The Moores had a second child, Daniel Killian Moore Jr. Both children were grown and married by the time Dan K. Moore became governor.

When her husband announced that he was going to run for governor, Jeanelle Moore was not excited. In fact, she did not want him to run. However, she became his most loyal campaigner and supporter. During the 1964 campaign, she traveled the state of North Carolina

Mrs. Moore square dancing with Willie York at a Southern Governors' Conference in Asheville

making appearances and giving speeches. At one point during the campaign, she accompanied the first lady of the United States, Lady Bird Johnson, aboard Mrs. Johnson's train, the Lady Bird Special, on a campaign tour of the state. Mrs. Johnson was impressed with Mrs. Moore's speaking ability and told her she would give anything to be able to speak impromptu with the ease of Mrs. Moore.

Upon Governor Moore's inauguration, Jeanelle Moore became an actively involved first lady. Before becoming first lady, Governor Terry Sanford had appointed her to the board of the North Carolina Fund to study the causes of poverty in the state. With an agenda of her own, she was the first governor's wife to have a full-time secretary and maintain her own office in the mansion.

In 1958, while her husband was a superior court judge, the Moores toured the Raleigh Correctional Center for Women. Mrs. Moore was dismayed to discover that the prison did not have a chapel. During Holy Week in 1966, the first lady launched a project to raise private funds to build a chapel. By December 18 of that year, with the majority of the funds in hand, groundbreaking ceremonies were held for the "Chapel of the Nameless Woman." In later years, Mrs. Moore would consider the place of worship her most cherished project.

Without Mrs. Moore's interest in and dedication to the North Carolina School of the Arts in Winston-Salem, that institution may never have been fully funded. After hearing the school's visionary first president, Vittorio Giannini, speak passionately about what such an institution would mean to students of the arts, Mrs. Moore vowed to assist the school in whatever way she could and convinced her husband and the legislature of its importance. From that time until her death, she poured her energies and talents into the school as a member of its foundation, its board of trustees, and as a friend. Governor Terry Sanford publicly acknowledged the fact that Governor and Mrs. Moore were responsible for the success of the school. In 1996 Mrs. Moore received the Giannini Award in recognition of her annual financial contributions to the School of the Arts, as well as for meritorious service to the institution.

Mrs. Moore's primary interest as first lady was the governor's residence itself. She quickly tired of the comments about the ugly gingerbread house on Blount Street. She was equally concerned with the deterioration of the interior of the building and the inadequacy of the furnishings and lack of proper décor. She called her first press conference at a luncheon only a few months into her husband's administration and announced the formation of the Executive Mansion Fine Arts Advisory Committee. Through that committee, the first lady hoped to increase awareness of the need to preserve the mansion and to promote its improvement through furnishings and works of art.

In 1965 there was a national movement toward historic preservation, as well as a renewed awareness of cultural resources in general. Mrs. Moore took advantage of that trend and called upon Lorraine Pearce, who had been the first curator of the White House and overseer of the redecoration of the White House during the Kennedy administration, to develop a plan to preserve North Carolina's executive residence. The Executive Mansion Fine Arts Advisory Committee held its first meeting on November 12, 1965, with Mrs. Moore and Mrs. Pearce in attendance. At Mrs. Pearce's suggestion, a tea was planned for June 20, 1966, with representatives of all one hundred counties invited. This event was a vital boost to a fund-raising campaign that would lead to the donation or purchase of major furnishings in the mansion's public rooms. The governor became involved with the first lady's interest in preserving the mansion. Governor Moore personally drafted legislation to establish the committee permanently as a state statutory committee, now the Executive Mansion Fine Arts Committee in the Department of Cultural Resources. Without Mrs. Moore's efforts to establish the committee and her ongoing interest in its mission to preserve the mansion at 200 North Blount Street, the house may well have been abandoned as the governor's residence in the last quarter of the twentieth century. Much of the current splendid beauty of the Executive Mansion is a lasting tribute to Jeanelle Coulter Moore.

Mrs. Moore announcing a statewide March of Dimes drive

As first lady, Jeanelle Moore had many other interests. She was said to be the busiest first lady in the state's history. She christened ships, a B-52 bomber named *The First Lady* at Seymour Johnson Air Force Base in Goldsboro, and the research vessel *Dan K. Moore*. She also headed the state's highway beautification program, later known as Keep North Carolina Beautiful, a venture that she would continue to support actively long after her term as first lady. Mrs. Moore was an advocate of tourism and of North Carolina's historic sites. She was especially active in the promotion of Tryon Palace and

Mrs. Moore and daughter Edith with Lady Bird Johnson

received a special citation from the Tryon Palace Commission for her work. Tradition was broken when she was elected president of the Sir Walter Cabinet while her husband was still governor. At the end of Governor Moore's term, a half-hour television program titled "A Tour of the North Carolina Executive Mansion with Mrs. Dan K. Moore" aired across the state. The program highlighted the results of her four-year labor of love and that of the Executive Mansion Fine Arts Committee.

Governor Moore and Mrs. Moore with President Lyndon B. Johnson at political convention (Robert W. Scott is shown behind Mrs. Moore)

After leaving the mansion, Mrs. Moore remained active in various causes and institutions. She was a trustee of the North Carolina Museum of Art and a member of that institution's education committee. When the art museum's new building was completed, she served as chairman of the dedication committee. She was both a trustee and a member of the executive committee of the North Carolina School of the Arts and a trustee of the Raleigh Boys Choir. Jeanelle Moore also served on Meredith College's board of advisers and on the board of directors of the Raleigh Rescue Mission. She received many honors throughout the years. The highest honor, however, was bestowed upon her and Governor Moore in 1980 when, together, they received the North Carolina Award for Public Service.

Governor and Mrs. Moore continued to live in Raleigh, where he was a North Carolina associate justice of the Supreme Court from 1969 until he retired in 1978. Daniel K. Moore died in 1986. Jeanelle Coulter Moore continued to be active until shortly before her death on October 20, 1999, at the age of eighty-eight. At her death Governor James B. Hunt Jr. proclaimed that "North Carolina has lost one of its strongest advocates of beauty and art." Mrs. Moore's funeral was held at Edenton Street Methodist Church, where she and her husband had been active since his election as governor. She was buried in Raleigh's Oakwood Cemetery alongside Governor Moore. She is survived by her son and daughter, three grandchildren, and eight great-grandchildren.

Jessie Rae Osborne Scott

1969–1973

OCTOBER 12, 1929

When Robert Walter Scott became governor, he was following in his father's footsteps. Robert Scott's wife, Jessie Rae Osborne Scott, became familiar with the role of first lady and the Executive Mansion during her frequent visits with his parents. Robert was attending Duke University when his father, W. Kerr Scott, became governor. He transferred to North Carolina State University and continued his courtship of Jessie Rae Osborne, which had begun in the fourth grade. When they married on September 1, 1951, they spent their wedding night at the Executive Mansion, and his parents honored them with a party.

Jessie Rae Scott, the youngest in a family of seven children, was born October 12, 1929, to Albert LeRoy and Rosa Cassidy Osborne. When she was eight years old, her mother died, and she moved from Massey Hill (near Fayetteville) to Swepsonville in Alamance County to live with her oldest sister. That mill village provided few employment opportunities for the bright young lady. Wanting to continue her education and encouraged by her employer and teachers, she worked and ultimately borrowed money from her future husband, which she paid back before the marriage, to attain that goal. With a degree in business education from Woman's College (now the University of North Carolina at Greensboro), she taught at Alexander Wilson High School, where she and Scott had been classmates and sweethearts. After their marriage, Robert Scott still had to finish his studies at NCSU and his military service, and she continued to teach for three years.

Life in their dairy-farm home changed with the arrival of five children. Twin girls, Mary Ella and Margaret Rose (Meg), were the first to arrive. They were born on February 18, 1956.

Governor and Mrs. Robert W. Scott with reporters on grounds of mansion

Susan Rae was born on April 3, 1957, followed by William Kerr on February 28, 1958, and Janet Louise on March 3, 1963. Having grown up in the midst of six siblings herself, Mrs. Scott was accustomed to the rigors of a large household.

Busily raising their children, Mrs. Scott also found time to grow vegetables, which provided food for freezing, canning, and preserving. The farm provided a wholesome environment for the children and gave them experiences with animals, plants, and a vast area in which to play. Mrs. Scott was active in the Hawfields Presbyterian Church, as her husband's family had been since its establishment more than two hundred years before. Her role in the community ranged from state Grange membership, to helping with the Red Cross bloodmobile and PTA fund drives, to chairing the state Cancer Crusade.

When her husband ran for lieutenant governor, Mrs. Scott set up an office in the house and worked on mailings, telephoning, and correspondence. In that way she was able to stay at home with the children and still assist her husband in achieving his political goal. During the gubernatorial race, however, with the stamina and dedication of a seasoned politician, she campaigned with her husband or took solo trips to give speeches and meet prospective voters.

Education was extremely important to Jessie Rae Scott. As first lady she supported her husband's program to make kindergarten part of the state's public school system. Since Mrs. Scott knew how important early education was for rural and small communities and that most residents of such places could not afford to send their children to private kindergarten, that issue became especially meaningful for the first lady. Mrs. Scott also produced a guide booklet for children visiting Raleigh and the governmental complex. Teachers and parents who accompanied the youngsters to Raleigh appreciated Mrs. Scott's effort to enrich the children's experiences in the capital. Once, during her tenure as first lady, Mrs. Scott substituted at Daniels Junior High School, probably embarrassing her daughter Susan, whose class needed a teacher.

Scott family portrait. From left, standing—Mrs. Scott, Susan Rae, Margaret Rose, W. Kerr, Mary Ella; from left, seated—Governor Scott, Janet Louise

Again focusing on children, the first lady, along with the State Library, held a "Story Festival" on the grounds of the mansion for more than one hundred children.

Mrs. Scott joined the state's Church Women United to raise fifty thousand dollars to match the General Assembly's appropriation for the expansion of the chapel at the girls' rehabilitation center at Samarcand Manor in Eagle Springs. Continuing her fund-raising efforts in 1971, Jessie Rae Scott held the first "pyramid party" to raise money for the North Carolina Symphony.

The first lady served as an ambassador for the state abroad. She traveled with her husband to France, Japan, and South America. In addition, she and some of their children visited Italy with the North Carolina School of the Arts summer program.

Mrs. Scott brought changes to the structure and holdings of the Executive Mansion. A playroom and billard table were installed in the unfinished third floor, providing a play area for the Scott children. The perimeter fencing, brick wall, and driveway gates were built with an appropriation following a plan devised during the Moore administration. Mrs. Scott oversaw the screening of the east porch and the redecorating of several rooms. At her encouragement, one hundred place settings of official state china were purchased, along with as many settings of silver-plated flatware.

Mrs. Scott toasting her husband on his fortieth birthday in the Executive Mansion Dining Room

The governor and first lady brought attention to the inadequacies of the Executive Mansion. The mechanical systems had been augmented in a piecemeal fashion over the eighty years since the mansion had been built. To garner support for the revitalization of the Victorian structure, they spoke of the feasibility of building a new official residence outside of the downtown area and turning the present mansion into a museum or an official guest house. Reactions were numerous and strong in the press and within the Executive Mansion Building Commission for some time. Eventually an appropriation was made to renovate and partially restore the Executive Mansion.

For the presidential inaugural ball in Washington, Mrs. Scott decided to show off one of the state's outstanding industries by wearing the newest man-made fiber, Dacron polyester—spun in Kinston, woven in Burnsville, and then fashioned into a dress by Doncaster in Rutherfordton.

Mrs. Scott hosting dinner for Dr. H. G. Jones's retirement

In a speech to the Raleigh Junior Woman's Club, quoted in the Raleigh *News and Observer*, Mrs. Scott summed up her beliefs: "'There are three kinds of doing,' she said. 'One is doing that that one has to do. Also important is doing what one wants to do. The third,' she continued, 'is altruistic—doing for another person. Much inner joy and satisfaction comes from service projects.'"

After her days as first lady, Mrs. Scott ran for political office as commissioner of labor but lost in the second primary. She then was employed for a number of years in the Department of Public Instruction in Raleigh, retiring in 1990. During those years her husband was president of the North Carolina Community College system. Melville Farms continued to grow and strengthen the family base in Alamance County.

Governor and Mrs. Scott have at least one politician among their children. In May 2000, Meg Scott Phipps (Mrs. Robert Eugene Phipps) won the Democratic primary for North Carolina commissioner of agriculture and consumer services. Her grandfather, W. Kerr Scott, had held the same position for eleven years, beginning in 1936, before he became governor in 1949. The family's dual legacy of agriculture and politics continues. During the campaign the former first lady baked for the campaign volunteers and worked in the office as time permitted.

It was said of this first lady in the January 1970 issue of the *Progressive Farmer*: "Few of us have begun our lives under less fortunate circumstances than did Jessie Rae Scott, and few of us can hope to attain such a position of honor, dignity, and responsibility as she now holds. But Jessie Rae Scott is truly a lodestar for North Carolina women to follow—especially rural women."

Patricia Ann Hollingsworth Holshouser

1973–1977

OCTOBER 29, 1939

Patricia Ann Hollingsworth Holshouser was well prepared for the rigors of being first lady. She had campaigned on behalf of her husband, James Eubert Holshouser Jr., in his successful bid to become the first Republican governor in North Carolina in the twentieth century. In addition, she had become familiar with Raleigh and state government while he served four terms in the state legislature just prior to his election as governor. Since they would carry the Republican platform to the forefront for the first time since Governor and Mrs. Daniel L. Russell (1897–1901), the Holshousers were conscious of the scrutiny they would receive.

As a minister's child and one of a pair of identical twins, Mrs. Holshouser was accustomed to being watched and thus was prepared to be in the public eye as first lady. These experiences gave her confidence and enabled her to assist the governor and carry out her duties. At thirty-three years of age, she had developed poise and a sense of self that would sustain her throughout their tenure.

Patricia and her twin, Nancy, were born in Asheville on October 29, 1939, to the Reverend Leon Howard Hollingsworth and Bessie Jo Walker Hollingsworth. Because Mr. Hollingsworth frequently moved from place to place as Baptist churches requested his services, the Hollingsworth family, which included the twins and their sister, Linda, lived in many towns, including Mebane, Boone, and Winston-Salem. The continual adjustment to new locations, schools, and friends contributed to the self-confidence of the future politician's wife and first lady.

While a nursing student at Wake Forest College, Patricia Hollingsworth began dating her future husband. She postponed her education to marry the young lawyer from Boone on June 17, 1961. Once settled into marriage, Mrs. Holshouser resumed her schooling and enrolled at Appalachian State University, where she earned a B.S.H.E. On September 27, 1963, their daughter, Virginia "Ginny" Walker, was born. Mrs. Holshouser taught sixth grade for one year in 1968 after her daughter entered school. By the time Mr. Holshouser was ready to launch his political campaign, Ginny was able to spend time with both sets of grandparents—the Holshousers in Boone and the Hollingsworths, who then resided in High Point—thus allowing her parents additional time to travel about the state.

After Governor Holshouser took the oath of office, he, Mrs. Holshouser, and Ginny settled into the Executive Mansion to begin their new adventure. Pat Holshouser knew that rearing their only child in the unique and unreal environment of the state's official residence was a mixed blessing. The Holshousers wanted their daughter to grow up in as normal an environment as possible, and they did what they could to bring that result about. Mrs. Holshouser continued to sew clothing for herself and her daughter, and she taught Ginny those skills as well. They also learned cooking and ceramic modeling. One of their great joys was using what they had learned to make Christmas presents.

Mrs. Holshouser cutting ribbon for Artrain *exhibition*

The General Assembly passed a bill in 1973 to renovate the Executive Mansion. With the persistence of the first lady, another bill for additional funding passed in 1975. That renovation and partial restoration was the largest and most extensive since the mansion was built. The cost was $854,806.70, largely spent on the mechanical systems—replacing the heating system, adding central air conditioning, recessing and changing the plumbing and electrical systems—and adding a fire escape for the second and third floors. With only about $35,000 designated for decorative elements, Mrs. Holshouser persuaded North and South Carolina textile companies to donate the materials needed to make draperies, for upholstering, and for carpeting. She used her sewing skills and with a group of volunteers and mansion prison staff created part of the window treatments. To make way for most of the work to be done, the Holshousers resided in a rented house from June 1975 to February 1976. When they returned to the mansion, Mrs. Holshouser hosted a party and viewing of the first and second floors for the workmen and the employees of the architectural and engineering firms. A color booklet was produced to publicize the newly renovated Executive Mansion.

Mrs. Holshouser dancing with children during Heritage Week

The bicentennial year brought many demands on Pat Holshouser. In preparation for that historic year, she hosted at the Western Residence a conference of first ladies from throughout the Southeast, led by Georgia's first lady, Rosalynn Carter. There the women formulated and organized upcoming celebrations. As a member of the board of directors of the Pines of Carolina Girl Scout Council, Mrs. Holshouser was also involved in their planning of bicentennial events. Girl Scouts from each of North Carolina's one hundred counties designed and created squares for a quilt and presented it to Mrs. Holshouser at the Executive Mansion. A spring trip to Ireland for the governors and first ladies from the thirteen original colonies was another highlight of 1976. For the holiday season, a tree featured in the Ballroom was decorated with handmade ornaments from North Carolina's schools for the deaf.

President Gerald R. Ford appointed Mrs. Holshouser to the National Council on Economic Opportunity, which worked directly with the Office for Equal Opportunity. Governor Holshouser supported his wife's advocacy of volunteerism in the state by creating the Commission on Citizen Participation and appointing her to head that body.

The Holshousers established a new home in Southern Pines after leaving the Executive Mansion. In an interview, the former first lady said that she "was ready to return to her role as wife and mother. I suppose I was also ready to renew my own identity as an individual with goals of my own." Mrs. Holshouser once again pursued her goal of becoming a registered nurse, one that she had set aside when she married. She received a master's degree in nursing from the University of North Carolina at Chapel Hill and worked at Moore Memorial Hospital in Southern Pines for several years. When former governor Holshouser's kidney problems became acute, his wife gave him dialysis treatments at home for six years before his kidney transplant.

Pat Holshouser continued her volunteer efforts by working with volunteer coordinators in Moore County. She also worked at Sandhills Hospice in Moore County and as patient care coordinator for Hospice in Scotland County. She found those jobs rewarding and challenging.

Mrs. Holshouser on scaffolding during mansion renovation

In 1989 Governor and Mrs. Holshouser participated in the marriage of their daughter Ginny to John Edward Mills Jr. and have enjoyed being grandparents to their granddaughters born in 1992 and 1994. Mrs. Holshouser's mother moved to Pinehurst, and the family spends a great deal of time together.

In reminiscing about her tenure as first lady, Pat Holshouser said that it "was really wonderful and it provided me with many opportunities to continue meeting the people of the state and to promote causes. . . . I will always remember those years as a special blessing."

Carolyn Joyce Leonard Hunt

1977–1985

JULY 3, 1937

Carolyn Leonard Hunt's tenure at the Executive Mansion was unique in North Carolina. Her husband, James Baxter Hunt Jr., was the first governor to be reelected to a second four-year term (1981–1985), a feat made possible by a change in the state's constitution approved by the citizens in 1978.

Carolyn Joyce Leonard Hunt, a native of Mingo, Iowa, was born July 3, 1937, to Carl Avery Leonard and Norma Henderson Leonard. She and her husband met at a National Grange Youth Conference in Hamilton, Ohio, when both were seniors in high school. He was serving as president of the North Carolina Grange Youth, and she was a member of the National Grange Youth Committee. Correspondence kept the romance alive. She attended Iowa State Teachers College until they became engaged. She then came to Raleigh, where she worked and earned an A.B. degree in primary education from the University of North Carolina at Chapel Hill. They were married on August 20, 1958, and had four children—Rebecca Joyce, born December 31, 1959; James Baxter III, born April 30, 1963; Rachel Henderson, born May 19, 1965; and Elizabeth Brame, born February 16, 1968.

In 1964 the Hunt family went to the Himalayan Kingdom of Nepal, where Mr. Hunt served as an economic adviser to that nation's government. During their stay, Mrs. Hunt taught in a school with an international student body and gave birth to their third child. After they returned to North Carolina, Mr. Hunt practiced law and in 1972 won election as lieutenant governor. He was first elected governor in 1976.

Carolyn Hunt was quick to admit that her family has always been her first priority. Each

Hunt family portrait. From left—Rebecca, Elizabeth, Mrs. Hunt, Rachel, Governor Hunt, Baxter

summer she and the children spent at least two months at their home, a farm near Rock Ridge in Wilson County, where life, according to Mrs. Hunt, "is that of a regular, everyday farm family." There the family maintained two gardens and Mrs. Hunt, who called the farm "our escape to normalcy," enjoyed freezing and canning vegetables. Her secondary interests included volunteerism, particularly the primary reading program. Her efforts as a volunteer inspired her husband, already an advocate of volunteerism, to develop an even deeper interest in the subject, leading him to create the Governor's Office of Citizen Affairs to promote volunteer initiatives. As chairwoman of the advisory council to that office, Mrs. Hunt gave support and leadership to volunteerism throughout the state.

While visiting an elementary school in Wilson County before her husband was elected governor, Mrs. Hunt had identified the need for aid in primary reading programs. Encountering a large class and the particular needs of one child for help, she decided to dedicate her spare time to the reading program. She devoted two days each week as a volunteer in the school and later helped organize the "Right to Read" project in Wilson County. As word of the program spread, more than two hundred volunteers joined the effort, which became the forerunner of similar programs throughout the state. Mrs. Hunt remained deeply committed to the project and, following her husband's election as governor, spent one morning each week at Wiley Elementary School in Raleigh assisting fifth-graders in reading and developing basic skills. She insisted that many more volunteers were needed for that task.

Another of Mrs. Hunt's special interests was the Friendship Force, an international exchange project with which she became acquainted at the National Governors' Conference in 1977. As she recalled her own positive experience as an exchange student in Germany, her interest in the program grew. She realized that the concept of families actually living together helped people to understand each other and contributed to world peace. In April 1979, as state chairwoman of the North Carolina Friendship Force program, Mrs. Hunt headed the project's first exchange. The family in Newcastle-upon-Tyne, England, with whom she and her youngest daughter spent ten days, later visited the Hunts in North Carolina. In part because of the success of that first exchange, North Carolina expanded its participation in the program.

Carolyn Hunt thought that the Executive Mansion was very beautiful, and early in her husband's administration she did little to change it except to increase the family's comfort by adding storm windows and dampers in fireplaces to help reduce draftiness. Later, however, she embarked on several projects for the residence. She suggested a revision of the statute governing the Executive Mansion Fine Arts Committee, and the General Assembly responded favorably. She then initiated numerous projects under the auspices of the committee, including renovation and redecoration of the mansion Library, where the woodwork was stripped and stained, and renovation and redecoration of the screen porch into a glass-enclosed Morning Room. Mrs. Hunt oversaw an extensive renovation of the institutional kitchen, the addition and furnishing of a first-floor waiting room, the installation of an automated lift at the front porch for use by handicapped guests, and the restoration and repair of antique furniture and the acquisition of many new pieces, including twelve matching Chippendale-style side chairs (which featured hand-made needlepoint seats made by ladies throughout North Carolina). She also located and framed photographs of all the first ladies who had presided over the mansion and continued the tradition of holding an annual holiday open house.

Mrs. Hunt tutoring children in reading

Governor and Mrs. Hunt's oldest daughter Rebecca was married to Jimmy Hawley at the Executive Mansion on October 20, 1979. For the historic event, Mrs. Hunt's sewing talents were on display in the form of two bridesmaids' dresses that she had made for the wedding. Previously, she had fashioned two of her daughters' dresses for their father's first inaugural ball.

Governor and Mrs. Hunt with daughter Rebecca and her husband, Jimmy Hawley, at their wedding in the Executive Mansion, October 20, 1979

For the four-hundred-year anniversary of the settlement of Roanoke Island, Mrs. Hunt christened the replica ship *Queen Elizabeth II* and hosted Her Royal Highness the Princess Anne of Great Britain and her entourage. In addition, she was responsible for the establishment of the Bailey-Tucker House as North Carolina's official guest residence in Raleigh.

During the eight years between Governor Hunt's service as governor, Mrs. Hunt continued to support the Friendship Force actively and led an exchange to Russia. She also served on the international board of directors and executive committee of Friendship Force International. In 1986 she was elected to the Wilson County School Board. However, her years as North Carolina's first lady were not yet completed.

Dorothy Ann McAulay Martin
1985–1993

JANUARY 21, 1937

Always ready for the next challenge in her life, Dorothy Ann McAulay Martin looked with anticipation to her role as first lady alongside her husband, Governor James Grubbs Martin. She remembered being told to be aware that each day she would be involved with history and that she and her husband were the stewards of the Executive Mansion and the office he held. These ever present thoughts kept her focused during their eight-year tenure. With effervescence and a contagious sense of humor, Dottie Martin could comfortably relieve the pressures in many situations. She was inspiring, intelligent, confident, strong, supportive, and energetic.

Born in Charlotte on January 21, 1937, to Benson Wood and Dorothy Louise Gill McAulay, Dottie Martin grew up there and in South Carolina. While attending a Presbyterian youth conference, she met her future husband, who was the son of a minister. She attended Queens College and the University of South Carolina before marrying James G. Martin on June 1, 1957. Dottie Martin worked in the Industrial Relations Department at Princeton University while her husband earned a doctorate there. They moved to Davidson, where he taught chemistry at Davidson College and she taught kindergarten from 1960 to 1972.

While in Washington, D.C., where her husband served as a congressman for twelve years, Mrs. Martin was devoted to rearing their three children: James Grubbs Jr., who was born on December 19, 1959, married Patricia Higgins, and had two children; Emily Wood, who was born on June 20, 1962, married Evan Richey, and had one child; and Arthur Benson, who was

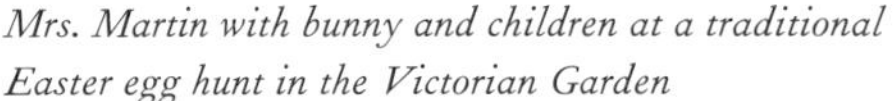

Mrs. Martin with bunny and children at a traditional Easter egg hunt in the Victorian Garden

Mrs. Martin picking up litter from highway

born on February 5, 1972. Mrs. Martin also worked as a real estate broker for seven years once the children were settled in school.

During and after campaigning for her husband's election as governor, Mrs. Martin set her sights and energy on the well-being and safety of children. In an interview she stated that for many years she had "growing concern for the changes that were affecting the family unit and particularly the children in our society." In order to enable parents to have their children fingerprinted, she encouraged the establishment of specially designated resource stations in twenty-one localities throughout the state.

She was most concerned about abused and victimized children and those with drug and sexually related problems. Mrs. Martin learned about the Parent to Parent program at a National Governors' Conference and established the program in seventy of North Carolina's one hundred counties. She received a national award for that achievement. Dottie Martin was also an active member of the Committee on Alcohol and Drug Abuse Among Children and Youth, which focused on the issues facing adolescents in our society.

Mrs. Martin continued her efforts on behalf of children when her husband appointed her to head both the Commission on Child Victimization and the Commission on the Family. From her perspective as leader of those two groups, she wrote, "Without the support, concern, and love of the family, our children fail to receive the care and guidance they need to become well-adjusted, responsible, and caring adults of the future."

After seeing plantings of wildflowers along highways in Texas, Mrs. Martin contacted the Department of Transportation to see if wildflower beds could be cultivated along North

Carolina's highways. The department began the program in 1985 and subsequently won a national award for their efforts. They then presented their award to the first lady in recognition of her inspiration in starting the successful program.

Upon her arrival at the Executive Mansion, Mrs. Martin noticed how much work was needed on the grounds. Several cold winters and dry summer seasons had caused damage. She raised funds, beginning with a grant from the Junior League of Raleigh, and eventually collected $185,000 to re-landscape the grounds of the mansion, especially the Victorian garden located on the south lawn. On May 27, 1987, that garden was dedicated to Mrs. Martin, "who through her love of nature, envisioned this enhancement to North Carolina's natural beauty." Public tours and an informative brochure on the garden and grounds were created under her direction.

The first telephone call received by Dottie Martin on the morning after the election was from Jeanelle C. Moore, who welcomed her to a small and unique club of women, those who serve their state as first lady. The two women built a genuine respect and friendship. When the centennial of the Executive Mansion was being planned, Mrs. Martin requested that Jeanelle Moore's portrait again be hung in the Ladies Parlor to recognize and honor her as the inspiration for establishing the Executive Mansion Fine Arts Committee. To mark the centennial, she encouraged the production of a historical video and book on the Executive Mansion and the establishment of a curator's office. In 1988 Mrs. Martin urged the committee to seek funds for the second century of the Executive Mansion and to establish the Executive Mansion Fund, Inc., a 501(c)3 nonprofit organization. By 1991, the mansion's centennial year, more than two million dollars had been raised.

Mrs. Martin delivering graduation address at Meredith College

After leaving the Executive Mansion, Dottie and James Martin lived in Charlotte and Lake Norman. Mrs. Martin was active in fund raising, serving on the board of trustees of Queens College, and the board of the Thurston Arthritis Center. She also was a hands-on member of the advisory board of the Family Center for Abused and Neglected Children, an organization dedicated to rebuilding the shattered lives of abused children and dysfunctional families—"A Place Where Hope Grows." Mrs. Martin's real joy was her three grandchildren's childhood.

As she reflected on her time as first lady, Mrs. Martin said that she was appreciative of the opportunities and that even though she "had not prepared for a life in the political spotlight, she had worked hard to make the most of it." She realized that from her position she could positively affect causes that interested her.

Carolyn Joyce Leonard Hunt

1993–2001

JULY 3, 1937

When Governor James Baxter Hunt Jr. and Carolyn Joyce Leonard Hunt returned to the Executive Mansion for an additional eight years, the voices of their children were replaced by the voices of their grandchildren. Mrs. Hunt, unique in having served as first lady for longer than any other woman in the state's history, was a pacesetter for North Carolina's women in their expanded roles of private and public life. Characterized as "an ordinary woman living in extraordinary life circumstances," Carolyn Hunt personified the changing role of first lady and of all the state's women. The wife, mother, grandmother, and volunteer activist changed, as did her role both in the home and within the statewide community. She helped to redefine the position of first lady from "helpmate" to leader in the realm of public service. Her increased involvement and independent participation in service programs brought a new level of professionalism to the position.

Mrs. Hunt was deeply committed to many programs, leading by example. Her strong convictions led her to fill leadership positions on issues of education, early childhood health, readiness for school, volunteerism, and women's health. Besides her weekly school volunteering, she worked in soup kitchens, hosted events for volunteers at the mansion, and regularly donated items to support fund-raising efforts. Representing her fellow citizens in highly visible projects, she demonstrated her fervent belief in community and community involvement. She was a regular tutor/mentor volunteer at Raleigh's Hunter Elementary and Carnage Middle Schools, making her teaching sojourns privately, working with her students without

Hunt family portrait. From left to right: front row—Katia Nilender; second row—James Hunt, Stephanie Hunt, Lindsey Hunt; third row—Deb Derrick, Elizabeth Amigh, Rachel Nilender, Joseph Hawley, Mrs. Hunt, Hannah Hawley, Rebecca Hawley; back row—Baxter Hunt, Kevin Amigh, Jonas Nilender, Olav Nilender, Governor Hunt, Jimmy Hawley; inset—Jackson Amigh.

fanfare, urging them to read aloud to her, and encouraging them to seek their full potential. Observers noted that she worked her magic quietly and lovingly.

In supporting Smart Start, her husband's unique early childhood educational model, Mrs. Hunt traveled to many counties, visiting day care centers, talking to care givers, and attending ribbon cuttings for openings of centers and offices. She likewise traveled on behalf of programs for senior citizens, school programs, and other public initiatives. She served as honorary chair of the North Carolina Partnership for Children, a job she took particularly seriously, always seeking ways to give Smart Start additional recognition. In conjunction with the national first ladies' initiative, she produced a children's literacy brochure individualized to North Carolina and distributed it through the Partnership, providing the organization with a tool to help children and families.

Mrs. Hunt served as a member of the advisory committee for the 1996 U.S. Women's Open golf tournament in Pinehurst to raise money for breast cancer research. For several years she prepared public service announcements on breast cancer awareness and spoke at a number of events promoting Breast Cancer Awareness Month. She believed that if she lent her name to a cause, she must take an active role and become personally engaged. JoAnn Norris, director

Mrs. Hunt with infants in day care center

of the Teaching Fellows Commission, remarked: "We love having Mrs. Hunt serve on this board. She always comes to meetings prepared. She offers sound suggestions and comments and is a real worker. She takes it seriously." Mrs. Hunt spearheaded a women's construction initiative, inviting female government officials and private citizens to volunteer in an effort to build a house for a homeless family through Habitat for Humanity's "First Ladies Build" program. She did real work—hammering, digging footings, and sawing.

To recognize Carolyn Hunt's two-decade commitment to its goals, the North Carolina Center for International Understanding (NCCIU; formerly the Friendship Force) created a teacher endowment in her name. Honoring the first lady's unceasing devotion to education at all levels, the Carolyn Hunt Teacher Endowment provides an annual award to state educators to participate in NCCIU educator exchanges. Millie Ravenel, director of NCCIU, remarked: "We are lucky in North Carolina to have as our first lady someone who can represent us with pride in the palaces of Paris or Beijing, but who is as real and down-to-earth as our next-door neighbor."

During her years in the Executive Mansion, Mrs. Hunt made visiting youngsters feel special. She initiated the practice of having schoolchildren's artwork displayed during tour seasons. In 1993 she implemented tours of the official residence for blind visitors. She opened the mansion gardens for seasonal tours and worked with the Executive Mansion Fine Arts Committee to fulfill its mandate to make and keep the residence an appropriate home for the state's governors and their families, as well as a center for official entertaining. Mrs. Hunt personally greeted thousands of visitors each year with warmth and southern hospitality.

Mrs. Hunt working with child in a Smart Start program

The Hunt family at daughter Elizabeth's wedding, September 9, 1995, which took place on the mansion grounds

While an avid supporter of her husband's very public political life, Carolyn Hunt was determined that her family enjoy a strong and private home life. She spent many hours each week in her public role and yet labored long and hard on the family farm. A highlight of Governor Hunt's third term was the marriage in the mansion garden of youngest daughter Elizabeth to Kevin Amigh on September 9, 1995. For the wedding, Mrs. Hunt, a talented seamstress, made outfits for five of the Hunt grandchildren, who served as attendants. During the last two terms, three of the Hunts' eight grandchildren were born, and Mrs. Hunt considered herself very fortunate to be present at each birth.

For Carolyn Hunt, inspiration came from the many people she met and places she visited on international trade missions with the governor. While in Israel, the Hunts met with Prime Minister and Mrs. Itzhak Rabin, who, like the first lady, were staunch advocates for children. Mrs. Hunt also visited several schools in Israel. At one elementary school she gave to Israeli students various articles from the Raleigh school at which she volunteered; the pupils from the two schools subsequently began a cultural exchange.

In the waning days of the final administration, Mrs. Hunt was touched by the sincerity of the many individuals who thanked her and Governor Hunt for devoting years of service to North Carolina. As she neared the end of her tenure, she reflected that her most inspiring memories came from watching and listening to the governor convince others to commit to projects, particularly Smart Start. "You realize that if you work hard enough and believe in a cause strongly enough," she said, "there is a way to make it become a reality." "I feel that my support, interest, and encouragement of such projects assists my husband in his accomplishments. You have to work together and maintain a strong commitment. There is no special training for these positions we find ourselves in. You lean on past experience. . . . I was raised to be very independent, and this has sustained me. Successes come through hard, hard work and many sacrifices, especially energy and time away from family."

As a rural girl from Iowa, Carolyn Leonard Hunt came to North Carolina as the bride of a young man reared on a family farm. Later in her life she dared the adventure of taking her young family to a remote country half a world away as her husband served as economic adviser to the government of Nepal. Mrs. Hunt shared and supported her husband's public life in the world of politics and government. She filled the post of first lady of the state during a momentous era in North Carolina's history and carved a path for other first ladies to follow in the new century.

Inaugural Ball Gowns

OF FIRST LADIES IN VARIOUS YEARS, 1889–2001

CORA WOODARD AYCOCK

Floor-length dress made by Worth of Paris,
with bustle, train, and accents of lace, embroidery, and appliqués

ELEANOR KEARNY CARR

Floor-length dress of taupe ribbed silk with velvet-and-lace trim, leg-of-mutton sleeves, and fitted waist

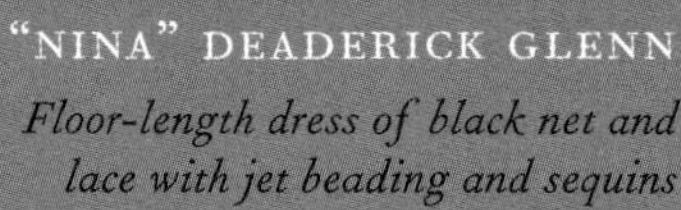

"NINA" DEADERICK GLENN

Floor-length dress of black net and lace with jet beading and sequins

ANNIE BURGIN CRAIG

Mid-calf-length dress of champagne silk chiffon with bugle beads and chenille embroidery

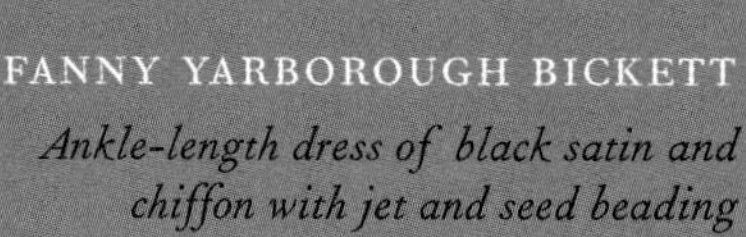

FANNY YARBOROUGH BICKETT

Ankle-length dress of black satin and chiffon with jet and seed beading

MARGARET FRENCH McLEAN

Mid-calf-length dress of gold and silver damask with hem flounce and accents of rhinestones, beading, and lace

FAY WEBB GARDNER

Dress of white velvet with gathered front inset, fishtail train; bodice accented with rhinestones

MATILDA HAUGHTON EHRINGHAUS

Bias-cut floor-length dress and matching jacket of gold brocade with rhinestone buttons and brooch

BESS GARDNER HOEY

Bias-cut floor-length dress of gold satin with train; overlay bodice edged with long fringe

ALICE WILLSON BROUGHTON

Floor-length dress of white silk chiffon with soft skirt and train; tucked bodice accented with rhinestone and brooches

MARY WHITE SCOTT

Floor-length dress of ivory velvet with side bustles and fitted waist; accents of lace and rhinestones

MERLE DAVIS UMSTEAD

Floor-length dress of blue chiffon with soft skirt; bodice and sleeves encrusted with pearls, rhinestones, and sequins

MARTHA BLACKENEY HODGES

Floor-length sheath dress of green lace and chiffon with pleated back panel

MARGARET ROSE SANFORD

Floor-length dress of pink silk with fitted waist and full skirt; accents of crystal beads and sprays of handmade flowers

JEANELLE COULTER MOORE

Floor-length sheath dress of embroidered white satin brocade

JESSIE RAE OSBORNE SCOTT

Floor-length dress of white and blue silk; bodice of lace encrusted with beading

PATRICIA HOLLINGSWORTH HOLSHOUSER

Floor-length dress of white and silver brocade with fitted waist and inverted front pleat

CAROLYN LEONARD HUNT

Floor-length dress of pale gold satin with gathered skirt and chiffon overlay; accented with chiffon bow at neckline

CAROLYN LEONARD HUNT

Floor-length dress of coral lace with layered skirt and lace rosette at waist

DOROTHY McAULAY MARTIN

Floor-length dress of red silk with full skirt and fitted bodice accented with chiffon rosettes

DOROTHY McAULAY MARTIN

Floor-length dress of turquoise silk with full skirt; fitted bodice with pleated caplet fastened with single rosette

CAROLYN LEONARD HUNT

Full-length tailored dress of copper metallic fabric with full skirt and fitted bodice

CAROLYN LEONARD HUNT

Full-length sheath dress of bronzed loden green velvet with copper ball and bugle beading, with floating collar.

First Ladies Prior to 1889
(1585–1889)

Researched and compiled by Debra A. Blake

Maiden names in italics

ROANOKE GOVERNORS

[Never married]
RALPH LANE
1585–1586

Tomasyn Cooper White
JOHN WHITE
1587

PROPRIETARY GOVERNORS 1663–1729

Sarah Prescott Drummond
WILLIAM DRUMMOND
1664–1667

Frances Culpeper Stephens (later Berkeley, Ludwell)
SAMUEL STEPHENS
1667–1669
MAY 1634–1690

[No record]
PETER CARTERET
1670–1672

Joanna [maiden name unknown] Jenkins (later Harvey)
JOHN JENKINS
1673–1676
DIED MARCH 27, 1688

[Name unknown]
THOMAS EASTCHURCH
1676–1678

[No record]
THOMAS MILLER
1677

Dorothy Tooke Harvey
JOHN HARVEY
1679
DIED DECEMBER 1682

Joanna [maiden name unknown] Jenkins (later Harvey)
JOHN JENKINS
1679–1681
DIED MARCH 27, 1688

Anna Willix Riscoe Blount Sothel
SETH SOTHEL
1682–1689
DIED BEFORE MAY 1695

Frances Culpeper Stephens Berkeley Ludwell
PHILIP LUDWELL
1689–1691
MAY 1634–1690

[Name unknown]
THOMAS JARVIS
1691–1694

Ann Dobson Archdale
JOHN ARCHDALE
1694–1696

Sarah Catherine Laker Harvey (later Gale)
THOMAS HARVEY
1696–1699
DIED CA. 1730

Ann Lillington Walker (later Moseley)
HENDERSON WALKER
1699–1704
JUNE 1, 1679–NOVEMBER 18, 1732

Martha Wainwright Daniel
ROBERT DANIEL
1704–1705

[Name unknown]
THOMAS CARY
1705–1706

Mary Davis Glover
WILLIAM GLOVER
1706–1708
DIED BEFORE 1707

Catherine [maiden name unknown] Glover (later Knight, Porter)
WILLIAM GLOVER
1706–1708

[Name unknown]
THOMAS CARY
1708–1711

Catherine Rigby Hyde
EDWARD HYDE
1711–1712
DIED 1738

Esther [maiden name unknown] Wilkinson Pollock
THOMAS POLLOCK
1712–1714
DIED 1716

Penelope [maiden name unknown] Golland Eden
CHARLES EDEN
1714–1722
1677–JANUARY 4, 1716

[Widower]
THOMAS POLLOCK
1722

Jane [maiden name unknown] Reed
WILLIAM REED
1722–1724

[Name unknown]
GEORGE BURRINGTON
1724–1725

Susannah Kidder Everard
RICHARD EVERARD
1725–1731

ROYAL GOVERNORS 1729–1775

[Name unknown]
GEORGE BURRINGTON
1731–1734

Penelope Golland Maule Lovick Phenney Johnston
GABRIEL JOHNSTON
1734–1752
DIED 1741

Frances [maiden name unknown] Button Johnston (later Rutherford)
GABRIEL JOHNSTON
1734–1752
DIED 1768

Mary Bursey Rice
NATHANIEL RICE
1752–1753
DIED CA. 1753

Elizabeth [maiden name unknown] Rowan Rowan
MATTHEW ROWAN
1753–1754

Justina Davis Dobbs (later Nash)
ARTHUR DOBBS
1754–1765
1745–DECEMBER 6, 1771

Margaret Wake Tryon
WILLIAM TRYON
1765–1771
CA. 1733–FEBRUARY 16, 1819

Elizabeth Martin Martin
JOSIAH MARTIN
1771–1775
1732–OCTOBER 1778

STATE GOVERNORS
1776–1889

Sarah Heritage Caswell
RICHARD CASWELL
1776–1780
1740–1794

Mary Whiting Jones Nash
(later Witherspoon)
ABNER NASH
1780–1781
1754–FEBRUARY 5, 1800

Mary Freeman Burke
(later Doherty)
THOMAS BURKE
1781–1782

[Never married]
ALEXANDER MARTIN
1782–1785

Sarah Heritage Caswell
RICHARD CASWELL
1785–1787
1740–1794

Frances Cathcart Johnston
SAMUEL JOHNSTON
1787–1789
1751–JANUARY 23, 1801

[Never married]
ALEXANDER MARTIN
1789–1792

Mary Jones Leech Spaight
RICHARD DOBBS SPAIGHT SR.
1792–1795
1765–MAY 4, 1810

Elizabeth Jones Merrick Ashe
SAMUEL ASHE
1795–1798
JUNE 10, 1735–JANUARY 3, 1815

Sarah Jones Davie
WILLIAM RICHARDSON DAVIE
1798–1799
SEPTEMBER 23, 1762–APRIL 14, 1802

Elizabeth Chauncey Jones Williams
BENJAMIN WILLIAMS
1799–1802
AUGUST 31, 1762–NOVEMBER 24, 1817

Ann [maiden name unknown] Cochran Turner
JAMES TURNER
1802–1805
DIED MAY 22, 1806

Margaret Polk Alexander
NATHANIEL ALEXANDER
1805–1807
CA. 1764–SEPTEMBER 13, 1806

Elizabeth Chauncey Jones Williams
BENJAMIN WILLIAMS
1807–1808
AUGUST 31, 1762–NOVEMBER 24, 1817

Hannah Turner Stone
DAVID STONE
1808–1810
1776–APRIL 1, 1816

Sarah Rhett Dry Smith
BENJAMIN SMITH
1810–1811
CA. 1762–NOVEMBER 21, 1821

Ann Swepson Boyd Hawkins
WILLIAM HAWKINS
1811–1814

Lydia Anna Evans Miller
WILLIAM MILLER
1814–1817
DIED MARCH 1818

Elizabeth Foort Branch
JOHN BRANCH
1817–1820
JANUARY 1, 1787–JANUARY 19, 1851

Maria "Meeky" Perkins Franklin
JESSE FRANKLIN
1820–1821
1765–FEBRUARY 20, 1834

Mary Smith Hunter Holmes
GABRIEL HOLMES
1821–1824
DIED 1838

Sarah Wales Jones Burton (later Joyner)
HUTCHINS GORDON BURTON
1824–1827

Frances Johnston Treadwell Iredell
JAMES IREDELL JR.
1827–1828
1797–OCTOBER 13, 1865

Lucy Ann Brown Owen
JOHN OWEN
1828–1830
SEPTEMBER 18, 1793–APRIL 19, 1853

Rachel Montgomery Stokes
MONTFORT STOKES
1830–1832

Eleanor White Swain
DAVID LOWRY SWAIN
1832–1835
APRIL 20, 1800–FEBRUARY 5, 1883

[Never married]
RICHARD DOBBS SPAIGHT JR.
1835–1836

Elizabeth Henry Haywood Dudley
EDWARD BISHOP DUDLEY
1836–1841
NOVEMBER 24, 1796–OCTOBER 23, 1840

Ann Eliza Lindsay Morehead
JOHN MOTLEY MOREHEAD
1841–1845
OCTOBER 14, 1804–JULY 29, 1868

Susannah Sarah Washington Graham
WILLIAM ALEXANDER GRAHAM
1845–1849
FEBRUARY 27, 1816–MAY 2, 1890

Charity Hare Haywood Manly
CHARLES MANLY
1849–1851
AUGUST 18, 1799–OCTOBER 22, 1881

Henrietta Williams Settle Reid
DAVID SETTLE REID
1851–1854
OCTOBER 7, 1824–MARCH 2, 1913

[Widower]
WARREN WINSLOW
1854–1855

Isabella Cuthbert Bragg
THOMAS BRAGG
1855–1859
DECEMBER 25, 1820–JULY 17, 1877

Mary McKinley Daves Ellis (later Nash)
JOHN WILLIS ELLIS
1859–1861
JANUARY 2, 1835–JANUARY 23, 1916

Mary Weeks Parker Hargrave Clark
HENRY TOOLE CLARK
1861–1862
MARCH 17, 1822–MAY 31, 1896

Harriett Newell Espy Vance
ZEBULON BAIRD VANCE
1862–1865
JULY 11, 1832–NOVEMBER 3, 1878

Louisa Virginia Harrison Holden
WILLIAM WOODS HOLDEN
1865
1830–MARCH 20, 1900

Martitia Daniel Worth
JONATHAN WORTH
1865–1868
OCTOBER 20, 1808–MAY 4, 1874

Louisa Virginia Harrison Holden
WILLIAM WOODS HOLDEN
1868–1871
1830–MARCH 20, 1900

Minerva Ruffin Cain Caldwell
TOD ROBINSON CALDWELL
1871–1874
JULY 19, 1820–JUNE 21, 1890

[Never married]
CURTIS HOOKS BROGDEN
1874–1877

Harriett Newell Espy Vance
ZEBULON BAIRD VANCE
1877–1879
JULY 11, 1832–NOVEMBER 3, 1878

Mary Woodson Jarvis
THOMAS JORDAN JARVIS
1879–1885
DECEMBER 12, 1842–FEBRUARY 22, 1924

Catherine Bullock Henderson Scales
ALFRED MOORE SCALES
1885–1889
MAY 27, 1845–APRIL 15, 1930

Appendixes

First ladies gathered at the Executive Mansion during Hoey administration, 1940. From left: standing—Mrs. Bickett, Mrs. Craig, Mrs. Kitchin; seated—Mrs. Broughton (wife of nominee for governor), Mrs. Hoey

First ladies with Hall of History display of first ladies' inaugural ball gowns and accessories. From left: Mrs. Hodges, Mrs. Gardner, Mrs. Ehringhaus, Mrs. Broughton

First Ladies, 1891–2001

Who Have Resided in the Executive Mansion at 200 North Blount Street

Helen Whitaker Fowle (Knight)
DANIEL GOULD FOWLE
1889–1891
JUNE 14, 1869–MAY 4, 1948

Louisa Matilda Moore Holt
THOMAS MICHAEL HOLT
1891–1893
OCTOBER 15, 1833–DECEMBER 9, 1899

William Eleanor Kearny Carr
ELIAS CARR
1893–1897
MARCH 1, 1840–MARCH 29, 1912

Sarah Amanda Sanders Russell
DANIEL LINDSAY RUSSELL
1897–1901
AUGUST 31, 1844–MARCH 18, 1913

Cora Lily Woodard Aycock
CHARLES BRANTLEY AYCOCK
1901–1905
OCTOBER 11, 1868–MARCH 13, 1952

Cornelia G. "Nina" Deaderick Glenn
ROBERT BRODNAX GLENN
1905–1909
SEPTEMBER 4, 1854–DECEMBER 9, 1926

Sue Musette Satterfield Kitchin
WILLIAM WALTON KITCHIN
1909–1913
MARCH 10, 1874–NOVEMBER 4, 1956

Annie D. M. Burgin Craig
LOCKE CRAIG
1913–1917
MARCH 15, 1873–NOVEMBER 6, 1955

Fanny Neal Yarborough Bickett
THOMAS WALTER BICKETT
1917–1921
OCTOBER 11, 1870–JULY 2, 1941

Angelia Lawrance Morrison (Harris)
CAMERON MORRISON
1921–1925
MARCH 24, 1912–JULY 13, 1983

Sara Virginia Ecker Watts Morrison
CAMERON MORRISON
1921–1925
MARCH 14, 1868–MAY 26, 1950

Margaret Jones French McLean
ANGUS WILTON MCLEAN
1925–1929
APRIL 29, 1879–NOVEMBER 1, 1959

Fay Lamar Webb Gardner
OLIVER MAXWELL GARDNER
1929–1933
SEPTEMBER 7, 1885–JANUARY 16, 1969

Matilda Bradford Haughton Ehringhaus
JOHN CHRISTOPH BLUCHER EHRINGHAUS
1933–1937
OCTOBER 23, 1890–JUNE 16, 1980

Margaret Elizabeth Gardner Hoey
CLYDE ROARK HOEY
1937–1941
JANUARY 21, 1875–FEBRUARY 13, 1942

Alice Harper Willson Broughton
JOSEPH MELVILLE BROUGHTON
1941–1945
JULY 13, 1889–AUGUST 15, 1980

Mildred Stafford Cherry
ROBERT GREGG CHERRY
1945–1949
AUGUST 8, 1894–APRIL 10, 1971

Mary Elizabeth White Scott
WILLIAM KERR SCOTT
1949–1953
APRIL 30, 1897–APRIL 23, 1972

Merle Holland Davis Umstead
WILLIAM BRADLEY UMSTEAD
1953–1954
JULY 11, 1901–APRIL 14, 1988

Martha Elizabeth Blakeney Hodges
LUTHER HARTWELL HODGES
1954–1961
SEPTEMBER 12, 1897–JUNE 27, 1969

Margaret Rose Knight Sanford
JAMES TERRY SANFORD
1961–1965
JUNE 6, 1918

Jeanelle Coulter Moore
DANIEL KILLIAN MOORE
1965–1969
JULY 13, 1911–OCTOBER 20, 1999

Jessie Rae Osborne Scott
ROBERT WALTER SCOTT
1969–1973
OCTOBER 12, 1929

Patricia Ann Hollingsworth Holshouser
JAMES EUBERT HOLSHOUSER JR.
1973–1977
OCTOBER 29, 1939

Carolyn Joyce Leonard Hunt
JAMES BAXTER HUNT JR.
1977–1985
JULY 3, 1937

Dorothy Ann McAulay Martin
JAMES GRUBBS MARTIN
1985–1993
JANUARY 21, 1937

Carolyn Joyce Leonard Hunt
JAMES BAXTER HUNT JR.
1993–2001
JULY 3, 1937

Foreword to the First Edition
of
The First Ladies of North Carolina

As I consider the proper content for introductory words to a book describing the lives of North Carolina's modern First Ladies, I am aware that my mind is full of varied images.

There is the image of gracious courtesy, so important in wives of prominent men. There is the image of selfless service, so much a part of women who have served their husbands and their states by working with cultural boards and commissions, volunteering in schools and leading charity fund drives. And there is, of course, the image of elegance, preserved in the delicate gowns we so eagerly admire when the North Carolina Museum of History displays its collection of inaugural gowns.

All of these are pleasant images, but they are flawed, I think, because they are soft, blurred generalizations lacking in the individual gifts and sparks which have made our First Ladies so very much a vital part of the history of North Carolina. What do these images tell us of the sturdy characters of women who stood side by side with governors? What hints do they give us of their background, their training and the achievements they carved out apart from those associated with their husbands?

Until now, we have had very few places to turn to fill in the smudged outlines of our images of our First Ladies. Thus, the publication of this volume is a most welcome event. It fills a gap that had become increasingly obvious as the concerns and accomplishments of women moved closer to the center stage of public attention. I hope, however, that this book will not serve as a final chapter in efforts to call more attention to North Carolina's women. Rather, I see it as a fine beginning, and I look forward to additional volumes focusing on other women of other times.

It is only fitting that the largest share of credit for this book goes to two women who have made their own rich contributions to the life of North Carolina. The name of Grace Hamrick is a familiar one to readers who appreciate a graceful phrase and a stylish sentence. She has given generously of her literary talents and her publishing expertise to insure that this project is completed with professional polish and historical accuracy.

And, of course, the entire effort bears the special stamp of that most special woman of North Carolina, Jeanelle Coulter Moore, wife of former Governor and Associate Justice of North Carolina Supreme Court Dan K. Moore. A truly elegant hostess and fiercely loyal helpmate to her husband through all the years of their marriage, Mrs. Moore is also in her own right an enormously active public servant, devoting her time and talents to dozens of causes ranging from the North Carolina Museum of Art to statewide beautification. Hers was the idea for this volume.

I knew Mrs. Moore as First Lady and I know her today as a friend. I look forward, as I know you do also, to finding more such remarkable friends within the pages of this book.

By Sara W. Hodgkins, *Secretary*
North Carolina Department of Cultural Resources

Foreword to the Second Edition of *The First Ladies of North Carolina*

Much has been written about the governors of North Carolina and their service to our state. The collections of governors' papers in the state archives contain detailed information on their varied participation in North Carolina's history. Numerous published studies focus on their lives and tenure in office.

Less is known of the wives of North Carolina governors. Yet the First Ladies of North Carolina have contributed importantly to the history and culture of the Old North State. Their first obligation, of course, has been as companions to their husbands. Each of us can recall images of our state's First Lady by her husband's side, a gracious and elegant hostess, or perhaps as his special representative at one function or another.

Because of their own interests the First Ladies have been active in education, the arts, and charities, and have served tirelessly on boards and commissions, often without the recognition they deserve.

In the present volume, *The First Ladies of North Carolina*, Jeanelle Coulter Moore, wife of former Governor and Associate Justice Dan K. Moore, and Grace Hamrick, Shelby journalist, have attempted, very lovingly and carefully, to fill in our knowledge of the twenty-five First Ladies who have lived in the present executive mansion since its construction in 1891. Together Mrs. Moore and Mrs. Hamrick have provided us with a welcome look at their lives and times. That they succeed so well is a tribute to them and to their desire to complement our understanding of North Carolina's rich heritage.

My hope is that this splendid book will continue to arouse interest in our history, the occupants of our state's highest office, and their First Ladies.

The First Ladies of North Carolina illustrates the finest qualities of the citizens of this state, in moments of celebration and joy as well as of tragedy. May North Carolina always be so blessed.

By Patric Dorsey, *Secretary*
North Carolina Department of Cultural Resources

Preface to the First Edition
of
The First Ladies of North Carolina

Much has been spoken and recorded about the governors of North Carolina, but historians seem to have avoided those gracious First Ladies who have, for the most part, been behind the scenes functioning as dutiful wives while their husbands have helped shape the history of the state.

On leaving the Mansion in 1968 after four active years as First Lady, Jeanelle Coulter Moore conceived the idea of a book on governors' wives. She pursued the idea for several years, garnering bits of information here and there and involving many people. Ideas have grown and the manuscripts have been rewritten and revised in a sincere effort to best present short biographies of each First Lady featured. Thus it was agreed upon that a more pleasing format would be one patterned after the edition of *The First Ladies of the White House*, a publication of the White House Historical Association.

Realizing it would be almost impossible to find sources of information for North Carolina's First Ladies prior to 1889, opinion evolved that those who had lived in the present Mansion would be the stars of this new book. Therefore, 24 First Ladies are featured on the ensuing pages beginning with Helen Fowle who served her widowed father as First Lady and was also first to occupy the Victorian Mansion in 1891. Actually the structure had been under construction for eight years and it was Governor Fowle's move that brought the project to completion . . . such as it was in those days.

The book concludes with lovely Carolyn Hunt whose historical role is that of an eight-year resident of the Mansion since her husband was reelected to a second term.

The short biographical accounts of the First Ladies are meant to portray their personalities and their accomplishments. Each is a celebrity in her own right, though early wives did not play the public role as society expects today. However, in researching their lives there is evidence of much brilliance and intellect among the attractive ladies. It is, in fact, almost a certainty that

Mrs. Grace R. Hamrick, Mrs. Carolyn L. Hunt, and Mrs. Jeanelle C. Moore holding first edition of The First Ladies of North Carolina

they have played a hand in this state's government alongside their illustrious husbands. They richly deserve their place in history.

It was my pleasure to become involved in this book some nine years ago when Jeanelle [Moore] and Sam Ragan (at the time secretary of the Department of Cultural Resources) commissioned me to write the biographies of Mrs. Clyde R. Hoey and Mrs. O. Max Gardner. Later Jeanelle requested that I write her biography, which also delighted me, and subsequently I was pleased to interview Pat Holshouser and Carolyn Hunt and record their interesting lives. I have taken the biographical material furnished me on the remaining 19 First Ladies and rewritten them to conform with the adopted new format.

I would like to make note of the fact that all of the time and energies and expenses I have put into this publication have been completely voluntary and I have received no remuneration. As the old cliche goes, it has been "a labor of love" and an effort I have thoroughly enjoyed.

My special thanks go to Mary B. Cornick of the Department of Cultural Resources who not only raised money for publication of this volume but whose support and confidence in me have been most appreciated. I am also indebted to Dr. William S. Price, Jr. and other personnel in the Division of Archives and History who compiled the list of First Ladies from 1776 to 1889.

Mrs. Moore, Mrs. Holshouser, and Mrs. Umstead signing the first edition of The First Ladies of North Carolina *in the Executive Mansion Ballroom*

Many other individuals throughout this state and beyond have aided in the compilation of this first book on wives of North Carolina governors and we owe them a debt of gratitude for their valuable information and research. Though it would be our wish to name each of these contributors, it would be an almost impossible task to present a total list since the book has been underway for several years. We do hope that partial repayment for their time and interests will be in the joy of seeing the book come to fruition. Too, we sincerely hope all sources have been accurate and we present the material as novice historians with strong intent to please each reader.

We do make note of the changing status of women in American life today and believe that volumes which will appear on the scene later will depict a different type First Lady . . . if not a lady governor!

Grace R. Hamrick
Shelby, N.C.
September 30, 1981

Preface to the Second Edition
of
The First Ladies of North Carolina

Much has been spoken and recorded about the governors of North Carolina, but historians seem to have avoided those gracious First Ladies who have, for the most part, been behind the scenes functioning as dutiful wives while their husbands have helped shape the history of the state.

On leaving the Mansion in 1968 after four active years as First Lady, Jeanelle Coulter Moore conceived the idea of a book on governors' wives. She pursued the idea for several years, garnering bits of information here and there and involving many people. Ideas have grown and the manuscripts have been rewritten and revised in a sincere effort to best present short biographies of each First Lady featured. Thus it was agreed upon that a more pleasing format would be one patterned after the edition of *The First Ladies of the White House,* a publication of the White House Historical Association.

Realizing it would be almost impossible to find sources of information for North Carolina's First Ladies prior to 1889, opinion evolved that those who had lived in the present Mansion would be the stars of this new book. Therefore, 25 First Ladies are featured on the ensuing pages beginning with Helen Fowle who served her widowed father as First Lady and was also first to occupy the Victorian Mansion in 1891. Actually the structure had been under construction for eight years and it was Governor Fowle's move that brought the project to completion . . . such as it was in those days.

The short biographical accounts of the First Ladies are meant to portray their personalities and their accomplishments. Each is a celebrity in her own right, though early wives did not play the public role as society expects today. However, in researching their lives there is evidence of much brilliance and intellect among the attractive ladies. It is, in fact, almost a certainty that they have played a hand in this state's government alongside their illustrious husbands. They richly deserve their place in history.

It was my pleasure to become involved in this book some 14 years ago when Jeanelle [Moore] and Sam Ragan (at the time secretary of the Department of Cultural Resources) commissioned me to write the biographies of Mrs. Clyde R. Hoey and Mrs. O. Max Gardner. Later Jeanelle requested that I write her biography, which also delighted me, and subsequently I was pleased to interview Pat Holshouser, Carolyn Hunt, and Dottie Martin and record their interesting lives. I have taken the biographical material furnished me on the remaining 19 First Ladies and rewritten them to conform with the adopted new format.

I would like to make note of the fact that all of the time and energies and expenses I have put into this publication have been completely voluntary and I have received no remuneration. As the old cliche goes, it has been "a labor of love" and an effort I have thoroughly enjoyed.

My special thanks go to Mary B. Cornick of the Department of Cultural Resources who not only raised money for publication of the first edition but whose support and confidence in me have been most appreciated. I am also indebted to Dr. William S. Price, Jr. and other personnel in the Division of Archives and History who compiled the list of First Ladies from 1776 to 1889.

Many other individuals throughout this state and beyond have aided in the compilation of this first book on wives of North Carolina governors and we owe them a debt of gratitude for their valuable information and research. Though it would be our wish to name each of these contributors, it would be an almost impossible task to present a total list since the book has been underway for several years. We do hope that partial repayment for their time and interests will be in the joy of seeing the book come to fruition. Too, we sincerely hope all sources have been accurate and we present the material as novice historians with strong intent to please each reader.

We do make note of the changing status of women in American life today and believe that volumes which will appear on the scene later will depict a different type First Lady . . . if not a lady governor!

Grace R. Hamrick
Shelby, N.C.
January 20, 1987

Bibliographic Essay

As in any work with a large scope, this book relies upon many sources. Primary sources included numerous private collections at the North Carolina State Archives, especially the Jeanelle Coulter Moore Papers. That collection consists of papers brought together during the preparation of previous editions of *The First Ladies of North Carolina*, by Grace Rutledge Hamrick and Jeanelle Coulter Moore. In addition to the private papers mentioned above, there were several collections at the Southern Historical and North Carolina Collections at the University of North Carolina at Chapel Hill. The Frank Porter Graham Papers, the William B. and Merle D. Umstead Papers, the Angus Wilton McLean Papers, and the Henry Groves Connor Papers were among the specific collections used. Other primary sources included federal census records, wills, estates, and death certificates available at the State Archives. Numerous Bible records were used as well. Some were provided by descendants of the first ladies; others were part of the Bible Collection at the Archives. First ladies' diaries were utilized when available. For the sketch on Helen Fowle, a death certificate from the Chicago Department of Vital Records and the records of Cave Hill Cemetery in Louisville, Kentucky, were consulted. Alumni records of many colleges and universities were used to verify attendance and graduation. The files of the curator of the Executive Mansion were likewise employed.

Few biographies of North Carolina's first ladies have been written. Grace R. Hamrick wrote two: *"Miss Fay": A Biography of Fay Webb Gardner* and *"Miss Bess": A Biography of Bess Gardner Hoey*. An unpublished biography of Amanda Russell is part of the Daniel Russell Papers in the Southern Historical Collection and was very helpful to the writing of her sketch. Surprisingly few biographies of the state's governors have been written, but the ones available were used extensively for this work. Among them are: Mary Evelyn Underwood's book about Angus McLean, *The Scotsman from Lumber River: Farmer, Industrialist, Banker, Public Servant*; Nancy Roberts's *The Governor*, about Governor Robert W. Scott; Jeffrey J. Crow and Robert F. Durden's *Maverick Republican in the Old North State: A Political Biography of Daniel L. Russell* and Durden's *Reconstruction Bonds & Twentieth-Century Politics: South Dakota v. North Carolina (1904)*; Oliver H. Orr Jr.'s *Charles Brantley Aycock;* Joseph L. Morrison's *Governor O. Max Gardner: A Power in North Carolina and New Deal Washington;* and Howard E. Covington and Marion A. Ellis's *Terry Sanford: Politics, Progress, and Outrageous Ambition*.

Helpful reference works located primarily in the Genealogical Services and Reference Services units of the State Library of North Carolina included: *Tombstone and Census Records of Early Edgecombe*, by Ruth Smith Williams and Margarette Glenn Griffin; *Register of the Commissioned and Warrant Officers of the United States Navy and Marine Corps*, published by the Navy Department; *Notable Southern Families, Volumes I–II*, by Zella Armstrong; *Washington County, Tennessee, Tombstone Inscriptions Plus Genealogical Notes*, by Charles M. Bennett; *Marriage and Death Notices in Raleigh Register, North Carolina State Gazette, Daily Sentinel, Raleigh Observer and News and Observer, 1867–1887*, compiled by Carrie L. Broughton; *Washington County, Tennessee, Wills 1777–1872*, by Goldene Fillers Burgner; *Sketches of the Shelby, McDowell, Deaderick, Anderson Families, Volumes I–II*, by Anna Mary

First ladies holding the state shell, the Scotch bonnet, on an outing to Manteo. From left: Mrs. Gardner, Mrs. Broughton, Mrs. Hodges, Mrs. Umstead, Mrs. Ehringhaus

Moon; *Alamance, the Holt Family and Industrialization in a North Carolina County, 1837–1900*, by Bess Beatty; *Edwin Michael Holt and His Descendants*, by Eugene Holt; *Development of the Textile Industry in Alamance County: "Evolution of Warp and Weft in Alamance,"* by Julian Hughes; *Fabric of a Community: The Story of Haw River, North Carolina*, by Gail and Robert Knauff; *Shuttle & Plow: A History of Alamance County, North Carolina*, by Carole Watterson Troxler and William Murray Vincent; *Centennial History of Alamance County, 1849–1949*, by Walter Whitaker; *Onslow Register: Record of Onslow & Jones Counties*, by Roger Kammerer and David Carpenter; *The Scott Family of Hawfields*, by Herbert S. Turner; *Hard-Circus Road: The Odyssey of the North Carolina Symphony*, by Benjamin Swalin; *The North Carolina Museum of Art: The First Fifty Years, 1947–1997, a Selected Chronology*, by Peggy Jo D. Kirby; and *North Carolina's Executive Mansion: The First Hundred Years*, by William Bushong. Several articles from the *North Carolina Historical Review* were useful in obtaining biographical information about first ladies. Lala Carr Steelman's "The Life-Style of an Eastern North Carolina Planter: Elias Carr of Bracebridge Hall" was especially helpful. Articles from *The State*, the *North Carolina Booklet*, and the *Dictionary of North Carolina Biography* were also consulted.

Contemporary newspapers were major sources of information, and many microfilm copies of them were used. The State Archives and the State Library of North Carolina provided most of them, and the rest were obtained through interlibrary loan. Used were: the Raleigh *News and Observer*, the *Raleigh Times*, the *Charlotte Observer* and the *Charlotte News*, the *Greensboro Daily News*, the *Greensboro Record*, the *Gastonia Gazette*, the *Goldsboro Argus*, the *Wilmington Morning Star*, the *Wilson Advance*, the *Salisbury Post*, the *Asheville Citizen*, the *Elizabeth City Daily Advance*, the *Scotland Neck Commonwealth*, the *Durham Morning Herald*, the Washington *Star*, the Winston-Salem *Journal* and *Journal and Sentinel*, the *Warren Record* (Warrenton), the *Mecklenburg Times* (Charlotte), the *Fayetteville Observer-Times*, the *Tarboro Southerner*, the Rocky Mount *Evening Telegram*, the *Alamance Gleaner* (Graham), and the *Monroe Journal*. The Chicago *Daily Tribune* and the Louisville (Kentucky) *Times* were especially helpful to the sketch of Helen Fowle.

Interviews with descendants were one of the best sources of information available, and both oral and written interviews were conducted. Interview notes left by Hamrick and Moore, as well as Beth Crabtree, were part of Moore's papers in the North Carolina State Archives and were especially useful.

Compiled and written by Debra A. Blake

Illustration Credits

NORTH CAROLINA DEPARTMENT OF CULTURAL RESOURCES:

N.C. State Archives:

pages v, 11, 13, 15, 16 (upper right), 17, 19, 20, 22 (upper right), 26, 30, 33 (both), 35, 38 (both), 39, 40 (both), 46 (both), 51, 57, 62, 63 (lower left), 69, 71 (lower right), 72, 73, 77, 79, 89, 97–98, 100 (left and lower right), 101 (all), 102 (upper left and middle right), 109, 110

Various Collections in the State Archives:

J. Melville Broughton Papers: page 49 (upper)

Jeanelle Coulter Moore Papers: pages 34, 65, 66, 68 (both)

Luther Hodges Collection: page 61 (lower right)

The *News & Observer* of Raleigh, North Carolina, Negative Collection: jacket (left); pages 31, 32, 41, 44, 50, 54, 55, 56, 58, 61 (upper right), 64, 67, 70, 82 (both)

N.C. Department of Agriculture: page 45, 49 (lower)

R. Gregg Cherry Papers: page 52

Alan Westmoreland and Bill Garrett:

endpapers; various scanned images and segments; various reproductions and enlargements

N.C. Museum of History:

Eric Blevins and Kent Thompson: pages 71 (upper left), 90–95, 100 (upper right)

NORTH CAROLINA DEPARTMENT OF TRANSPORTATION:

Charles E. Jones: page 85 (upper)

UNIVERSITY OF NORTH CAROLINA LIBRARY, CHAPEL HILL:

North Carolina Collection: Angus Wilton McLean Papers: page 37

EAST CAROLINA UNIVERSITY, JOYNER LIBRARY:

Special Collections Department: Elias Carr Papers: pages 4 (both), 16 (lower left)

HAW RIVER HISTORICAL MUSEUM:

page 14

PERSONAL COLLECTIONS:

Bickett Family Collection: pages 27, 28, 29

Broughton Family Collection: pages 47, 48, 114

Ehringhaus Family Collection: page 43

Glenn Family Collection: pages 21, 22 (upper left)

Hodges Family Collection: page 60

Holshouser Family Collection: pages 74, 75, 76

Hunt Family Collection: pages 80, 84, 85 (inset), 86 (upper left), 87

Kitchin Family Collection: pages 23, 24

McLean Family Collection: page 36

Martin Family Collection: page 81

Moore Family Collection: page 66

Sanford Family Collection: page 63 (upper right)

Worth Family Collection: page 102 (lower left)

THE *NEWS & OBSERVER* OF RALEIGH, NORTH CAROLINA:

pages 83, 86 (lower right)

EXECUTIVE MANSION CURATOR'S OFFICE:

jacket (front and back edge and inside flaps); pages 25, 42, 53, 59, 78, 81

Leslie Wright Dow: jacket (right and lower middle); pages 7 (both), 10

Index

lice W. Broughton Sarah Amanda Cora
ildred.
Annie B. Craig Jeanelle C. Moore
gelia
Carolyn L. Hunt Matilda
Annie B. Craig Mrs. T. W.
orothy M. Martin
Mrs. T. W. Bickett
Jessie Rae Scott
Mildred
Musette Kitchin
Pat Mrs. Clyde R. Hoey. Do
Merle Davis Umstead Fay Webb
Deaderick Glenn.
Sarah Amanda
Mary Sall
Jessie Rae Scott
Carolyn Hunt
rt Fowle
Margaret Rose Sanford
Margaret F. McLean
Mrs. T.
Jessie Rae Scott
Laura Ecker Mo